GREAT DESIGN

USING 1, 2, & 3 COLORS

Red
160

To Mom and Dad

Thanks to all the designers who submitted their works. Special thanks to the staff at Supon Design Group —
Andy, Dianne, Dave, Wayne, Rick, and Tony — who helped realize this book's smooth completion.
To Linda Klinger and Bradley Rymph for their writing. And to Jerry McConnell, for his wisdom.
— Supon Phornirunlit

Distributors to the trade in the United States and Canada:

F & W Publications, Inc.
1507 Dana Avenue
Cincinnati, Ohio 45207

Distributed throughout the rest of the world by:

Hearst Books International
1350 Avenue of the Americas
New York, NY 10019

Publisher:

Madison Square Press
10 East 23rd Street
New York, NY 10010

Great Design Using 1, 2, & 3 Colors **is a project of:**

Supon Design Group, Inc.
International Book Division
1000 Connecticut Avenue, NW, Suite 415
Washington, DC 20036

ISBN 0-89134-502-7

Printed in Hong Kong

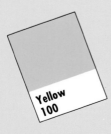

ACKNOWLEDGMENTS

Art Director and Editor

Supon Phornirunlit

Managing Editor

Wayne Kurie

Writers

Linda Klinger
Bradley Rymph

Design Editors

Andrew Dolan
Supon Phornirunlit

Assistant Art Directors

Dianne Cook
Andrew Dolan

Designer

Andrew Dolan

Supporting Staff

Rick Heffner
Dave Prescott
Tony Wilkerson

Desktop Publishing

microPRINT, Washington, DC

Camera Services

Quadrant Slide Services

Orange
148

TABLE OF CONTENTS

Purple
514

The business of graphic design—like that of any art—is built on a foundation called subtlety. Although the message may pack a powerful punch, good design concepts don't grandstand and are not meant to leap off the page. The type, the position of the words, the tilt of an illustration, and the boldness of a line all work behind the scenes, and seldom receive an encore. Often, only those in the industry can recognize the careful choice of components that result in the overall, effective picture.

But it is subtleness—the insight that communicates so much with so little—that, time and again, becomes key in award-winning design. And nowhere is that subtleness used with more precision than in the often untouted art of restricted color use.

The approximately 170 design creations included in *Great Design Using 1, 2, & 3 Colors* demonstrate the quality products that are possible with a limited number of colors, as well as the emerging popularity of using relatively few colors in print design. Clearly, limited color often results in an appeal unachievable when using a rainbow of shades.

A vital part of design, of course, is color. Color can add shape to a formless thought and interest to an unpopular message. So why would a designer with virtually hundreds of combinations available to him or her choose to restrict the use of color on a print piece? The wide range of exceptional work in this book gives just a few impressive reasons.

When color is used, to paraphrase Matisse, the level of energy brought out in design is almost supernatural. But there must be precision in restricted color: When fewer colors are used, each hue becomes bolder, stronger, and more vital. Each design component appears to work harder to achieve the desired effect. In the pages of this book, we've included a variety of graphics projects, from stationery to product packaging to signage, demonstrating admirable resourcefulness and imagination. Each color truly seems to possess an intense force. A single color becomes an identity-builder when used throughout a campaign. A second color, when carefully chosen and placed, renders a vivid quality to the design elements, or builds contrast. A third color, in turn, highlights a distinctive element, or neatly ties a masthead to a page. With so much less to distract the eye, the result often becomes startlingly effective.

And the eye, occasionally, even plays tricks on the viewer. Many times, I was surprised at the completeness and complexity of the message delivered in the works we had chosen, and actually had to re-count to ensure that only three or fewer colors were used as agents. Somehow, it seemed three or fewer colors had played the role of an entire palette—rendering a powerful energy that indeed bordered on magic.

Red
191

Sometimes the choice to restrict color is requested by clients whose design work must be crammed into a small budget. A few designers still balk at a one-, two-, or three-color limit, feeling it confining and stifling of creativity. How often I've heard designers scoff, "High design appeal from a low budget? That's too difficult!" But after assembling this book, I feel the difficulty comes only in the way we approach the task. Restricted color use trains the designer to rein in his or her scattered creative thoughts. I believe it actually teaches us to focus.

But the pieces in this book also demonstrate that restricted color usage is not limited to low-budget projects. Sometimes designers limit their use of different inks simply because they intuit that the pieces they are developing need the variety and vibrancy that come from precisely screening and creatively blending just a few inks or elements.

A multitude of techniques can be used when designing with three or fewer colors, but all demand thoughtful planning. Sometimes the paper itself is used as one color—or, in packages with more than one piece (for example, stationery), different paper stocks may be used with different pieces to give even more color variety. This technique must be applied carefully, however: Even though vibrant colors do increase paper opacity, they may also decrease legibility, because contrast between background and type can be compromised.

At times, design pieces are technically classified as having one, two, or three colors because they were printed on a press with that number of ink fountains—but they may actually contain more ink colors. Graphic designers are increasingly making use of the incredible variety that can be achieved by using a "split fountain"—that is, by filling a printing press's fountain with more than one color of ink. One of this volume's "two-color" entries used black ink in one fountain and *five* different inks in the other . Another entry that we've included used two inks in one fountain and three inks in the second.

Manual "tricks" may also be used to enhance the creativity and effectiveness of a design piece. Among the entries included in this volume are a stationery package and a birth announcement that get extra color because of handstamping each piece; stationery packages and a poster that include manual cutting to get their unique shapes; a poster printed in newsprint that is then crumpled for added effect; and black-ink posters for a repertory theater company to photocopy as needed.

Then there's the selection of the colors themselves. We've all learned how certain colors quietly convey strong messages. Green is popular for financial or ecological themes; blue or bronze connotes success or a conservative image. But just page through this book to see how rules can be broken. Siren red can be used from everything from an Italian restaurant identity campaign to the childlike crayon scribbles of a day care center. Not surprisingly, black is the most commonly used ink among the entries in this book. Red, in its various shades, is the second most popular color.

In graphics, designers are forever renewing what has otherwise grown commonplace, coaxing an additional thought, a new approach, an unusual twist out from the old. Both liberal color use and color restriction are powerful elements used to breathe life into a weary idea. But fewer colors often say much more using the same space.

When we released our call for entries for this volume, we were deluged with over 2,000 submissions from 16 countries. After making our first cut, we still had over 500 possible entries. The 168 entries that were finally selected came not only from industrialized countries famous for their graphic design—the United States, Canada, Switzerland, Japan, etc. Many also came from developing or newly independent countries, such as Mexico, Poland, Croatia, and Slovenia.

All these design pieces demonstrate fresh thoughts and unusual innovation. There are lessons forever to be learned when studying design from different countries. They remind us that thought-provoking qualities are attributed to the richness of each culture and often can be found nowhere else.

This book offers proof that low budgets restricting use of color don't have to mean poor design results. Each piece we've included underscores a different effect, and offers another reason to consider using a limited color approach, even when budgets are more than accomodating. The effect is immediately dramatic, and often colors seem brighter and more expressive—something to consider before automatically reaching for your color-swatch book.

There is an old adage which states that less is more. In graphics, simplifying the design can indeed add a great deal of power to what's already there. We hope we've given you many ideas that will help you focus your message.

Supon Design Group's International Book Division takes great pleasure in presenting *Great Design Using 1, 2, & 3 Colors* — the first volume in what we hope will be a series of publications presenting the best limited-color print design from around the world. We invite your comments and also hope you will consider submitting entries for our next publication. Simply fill in the postcard enclosed with this book and return it to us.

Graphically yours,

Supon

Supon Phornirunlit

Blue
265

Owner and art director of the Washington, D.C.-based Supon Design Group, Inc., Supon was born in Bangkok and studied design in Thailand, and the United States. Currently, Supon is on the board of directors of the Art Directors Club of Metropolitan Washington and is project director of the Washington Trademark Design bi-annual competitions. Since opening his studio in 1988, Supon has been featured in several publications, including the Washington *Journal* of AIGA, *HOW's 1990 Business Annual, Designers' Self Image,* and *Asia's Media Delite.* In the past four years, Supon has earned over 200 awards from the Art Directors Clubs of both New York and Washington, AIGA, Type Directors Club, American Corporate Identity, DESI, Print's Design Annual, and many others. His studio has authored several books exploring the nuances of graphic design, such as *Design in Progress* and *International Logos & Trademarks,* and its work has been exhibited in England, Germany, Israel, Japan, Thailand and the United States.

ONE

Yellow
105

COLOR

Schaffer's Bridal Shop
Identity

DESIGN FIRM
Sayles Graphic Design
(Des Moines, Iowa)

ART DIRECTOR
John Sayles

CLIENT
Schaffer's Bridal and Formal Wear

What was
your favorite
part of our
wedding?

When you
were coming
down the aisle.

Really?
Why?

Because you
were coming
down the aisle
for me.

Schaffer's Bridal and Formal Shop 1994

In preparing a coordinated graphic identity for Schaffer's Bridal Shop, designer John Sayles created a logo featuring a stylized "S" and complementary brushstroke. These graphics were applied not only to the shop's stationery but also to posters, hat and clothing boxes, and other materials. Suggesting the formality appropriate to a bridal shop, all items used black ink only on white (except for a sweatshirt, with a touch of gold). Store materials were printed on white parchment; a printed pattern on the second side showed through, creating a screenlike look.

Russ Rogers, Wood Craftsman
Stationery

DESIGN FIRM
Patrick Mountain Advertising &
Graphic Design
(Los Gatos, California)

ART DIRECTOR
J. Robert Faulkner

CLIENT
Russ Rogers, Wood Craftsman

Printed on light beige, flecked paper stock and featuring a curled, thin splice of paper across the top, this letterhead by designer J. Robert Faulkner graphically suggests the wood shavings characteristic of Russ Rogers' trade. Rogers creates the splice of paper by cutting and rolling it himself after typing each letter.

Lynn Tanaka Illustration
Stationery

DESIGN FIRM
Lynn Tanaka
(Minneapolis, Minnesota)

ART DIRECTOR
Lynn Tanaka

CLIENT
Lynn Tanaka

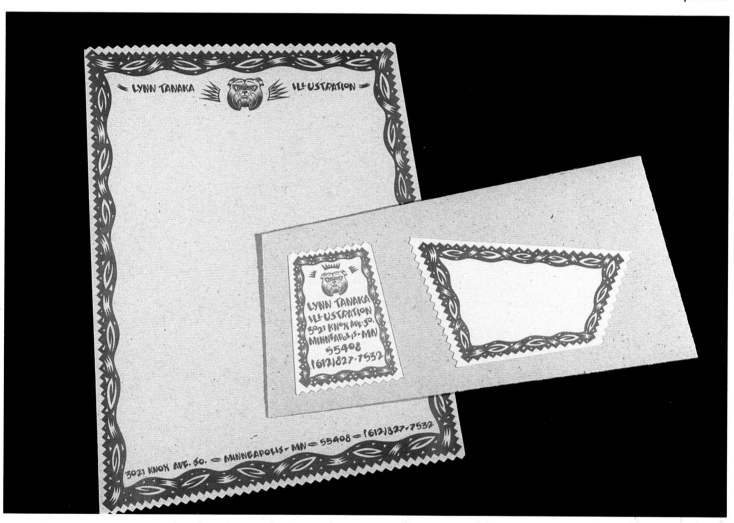

Illustrator Lynn Tanaka went for a unique look when she used trapezoidal, rather than standard rectangular, shapes for her stationery package. All elements in the package are hand-cut, with pinking shears used for the notched edges. The hand-made envelope's return address and space for typing in the addressee's name are pasted-down copies of her business card and shipping label.

Utopia
Stationery

DESIGN FIRM
Ideas
(San Francisco, California)

ART DIRECTOR
Robin Brandes

ILLUSTRATOR
John Hersey

CLIENT
Hammersly Technology Partners

Despite its use of only black ink, this stationery for a computer software developer remains eye-catching with its yellow paper stock and relatively subdued logo.

Lisa M. Brzezniak
Stationery

DESIGN FIRM
Lisa M. Brzezniak, Graphic Designer
(Washington, D.C.)

ART DIRECTOR
Lisa M. Brzezniak

CLIENT
Lisa M. Brzezniak

Designer Lisa M. Brzezniak
used various misspellings of
her last name to make her
letterhead and envelope
distinctive. By using a red
marker to indicate the
correct spelling, she adds a
two-color effect to the black-
ink-only stationery.

Helmut Schmid
New Year's Card

DESIGN FIRM
Helmut Schmid Design
(Osaka, Japan)

ART DIRECTOR
Helmut Schmid

SUIBOKU (BRUSH WORK)
Sumi Schmid

CLIENT
Helmet Schmid Design

In recent years, designer Helmut Schmid's New Year's cards have incorporated quotations that make an impression on him. On this card for 1991, he used a line by the Austrian poet Peter Handke ("I will only just say what I can say in one breath") and intensified the saying with a suiboku brush work expressing the same philosophy.

Detter
Christmas Card

DESIGN FIRM
Detter Graphic Design
(Madison, Wisconsin)

ART DIRECTOR
Jeanne Detter

CLIENT
Detter Graphic Design

The integration of a handmade paper from southern France as part of the design gives a unique look to this Christmas card for designer Jeanne Detter. The stock did cause some production challenges because of its fiber, and sometimes the ink lifted off completely.

Wohnflex
Invitation

DESIGN FIRM
BBV Baviera
(Zürich, Switzerland)

ART DIRECTOR
Michael Baviera

CLIENT
Wohnflex

This invitation card for a Swiss boutique for modern design furniture was produced by creating a new graphic design that was then printed on paper that had already contained print.

Collins
Birth Announcement

DESIGN FIRM
Collins & Chu
(Tustin, California)

ART DIRECTOR
Bill Collins

DESIGNERS
Bill Collins, Lorna Moy-Masaki

CLIENT
William Hayes Collins

Here's the Poop!

Bill and Pauline Collins
are proud to announce:
It's a Billy Boy!
William Hayes Collins
born December 20, 1990
at 6:59 PM
7 pounds 12 ounces
21 inches long.

Designer Bill Chu prepared this announcement for the birth of his son. The 5"x9" announcement folded into the shape of a diaper to fit in a custom-cut envelope secured by a safety pin.

■

VR Graphics
Self-Promotion

DESIGN FIRM
VR Graphics / Communications
(La Canada, California)

ART DIRECTOR
Vince C. Rini

CLIENT
VR Graphics / Communications

A variety of paper colors and stocks, including a corrugated cardboard folder, combine to give a multicolored look to this black-ink-only packet promoting designer Vince Rini's studio.

Eymer Design
Stationery

DESIGN FIRM
Eymer Design
(Boston, Massachusetts)

ART DIRECTORS
Douglas Eymer, Selene Carlo-Eymer

ILLUSTRATOR
Douglas Eymer

CLIENT
Eymer Design

Eymer Design adds color as well as individuality to each item in its stationery package by printing the various elements on different paper stocks and by manually applying rubber stamps to them. Some pieces, such as the business card and mailing label, are printed with black ink. Other pieces, including the letterhead and no. 10 envelope, are not run through a printing press at all. An added benefit of this approach, in the words of Douglas Eymer, is that the manual stamping provides "great stress relief."

Vaucluse House Tearoom
Identity

DESIGN FIRM
Annette Harcus Design
(Double Bay, New South Wales, Australia)

ART DIRECTOR
Annette Harcus

CLIENT
Vaucluse House Tearoom

By using ornate frames and screened illustrations, designer Annette Harcus gave an elegant look to the menus and related materials for the Vaucluse House Tearoom — an art deco cafe set within the gardens of a historical home. The menu, produced on a small budget, had to have a flexible design and be easy to update. In addition, the overall graphic identity needed to include a memorable image that could extend onto souvenir items such as postcards and T-shirts.

MENU

Rockfish soup with rouille & croutons	5.50
Roasted tomato & farmhouse cheese on Bruschetta	6.50
Braised duck leg, red cabbage & apple	9.00
Prawn lasagne with vegetable butter	10.00
Salad of ginger cured tuna, avocado, tomato & sesame dressing	8.00
BBQ pork & chinese noodle salad	8.00
Bresaola, goat's cheese & bitter greens	8.00
Roasted rack of lamb, ratatouille & pesto	15.00
Veal medallion and mushroom risotto	15.00
Poached chicken breast with potato leeks & Chinese mushrooms	14.50
Rare roast beef fillet with Yorkshire pudding	15.00
Duck breast & quince with red wine sauce	16.00
Cassoulet of goose, pork sausage & white beans	15.50
Today's Fish ~ please ask your waiter	

Caesar Salad 7.00   Steamed Vegetables 4.00

WINES

~ Tyrrells Glenbawn Semillon N.S.W.	12.00/3.00 glass
rgundy N.S.W.	14.00
ry White WA.	20.00
W.	25.00
esling S.A.	15.30
N.S.W.	14.00
W.	16.50
S.A.	25.00
e ~ Croser Pine Ridge S.A.	13.00/4.50 glass
ic.	25.00
y N.S.W.	14.00
128 S.A.	15.00
N.S.W.	16.50
a Bitter Beer	4.00
~ Muscat	4.00

AUCLUSE HOUSE TEAROOMS

Licensed

Wentworth Road, Vaucluse, NSW 2030

Open Tuesday to Sunday 10 am ~ 5 pm

(except Public Holidays, Good Friday & Christmas Day

nd & Public Holiday Surcharge $1.00 per adult

ke free area and for the comfort of our guests, no pipes or cigars

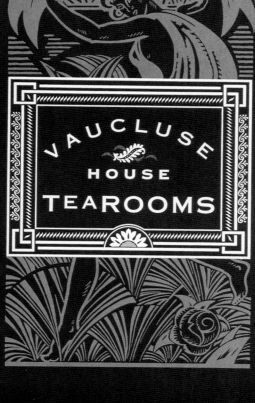

L'OTEL
Identity

DESIGN FIRM
Annette Harcus Design
(Double Bay, New South Wales, Australia)

ART DIRECTOR
Annette Harcus

CLIENT
L'OTEL

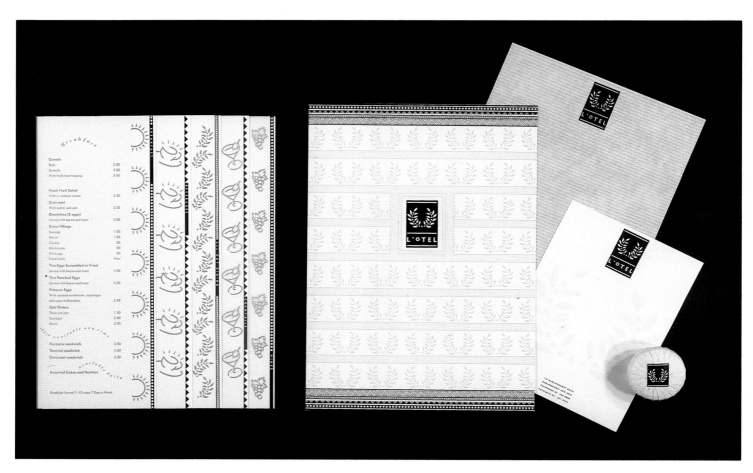

Despite a very small budget, L'OTEL, a small boutique hotel and restaurant, needed a graphic identity that presented a stylish, fashionable image. To give added elegance to L'OTEL's stationery, designer Annette Harcus used screens of the logo as a subdued background effect. She also gave distinctive identity to various portions of the restaurant's menu by creating simple illustrations and printing them down each sheet's right margin.

Published for faculty, staff, alumni, and friends of the Fashion Institute of Technology

Network

F.I.T.

Volume Two, Number Two
Winter 1992

F.I.T. Network
Newsletter

DESIGN FIRM
Richard Danne & Associates
(New York, New York)

ART DIRECTORS
Richard Danne, Gary Skeggs

DESIGNERS
Gayle Shimoun, Gary Skeggs

CLIENT
Fashion Institute of Technology

By blending crisp halftones of various shapes and sizes with a clear grid and multiple typestyles, this quarterly newsletter for New York's Fashion Institute of Technology has a cover that quickly and attractively demands attention.

Food for Thought
Self-Promotion

DESIGN FIRM
Value Added Design
(Fitzroy, Victoria, Australia)

ART DIRECTOR
Heather Towns-Cook

DESIGNERS
Heather Towns-Cook, Anton Banuski

CLIENT
Value Added Design

For a studio promotion, Value Added Design prepared jars of chocolate candies with a label describing the "ingredients" the studio provides to give relief from design worries. A corrugated cardboard package for the jars includes glued-on illustrations of famous thinkers on the outside and a copy of the studio's design philosophy (accompanied by illustrative quotations) on the inside. All papers used for the promotion were recycled stock.

Reed Design
Self-Promotion

DESIGN FIRM
Reed Design Associates
(Madison, Wisconsin)

ART DIRECTORS
Gail Bothum, Stan Reed

DESIGNER
Gail Bothum

WRITER
John Besmer

CLIENT
Reed Design Associates

This promotional package included a battery-operated clock on corrugated plastic, accompanied by folders containing a calendar for each month of the year. The date numbers for each week were printed on separate plastic strips for the recipient to slip into the clock's corrugated slits. An additional plastic strip, already inserted into the clock, noted the recipient's name.

IBM Switzerland
Book Jacket

DESIGN FIRM
BBV Baviera
(Zürich, Switzerland)

ART DIRECTOR
Michael Baviera

CLIENT
IBM Switzerland

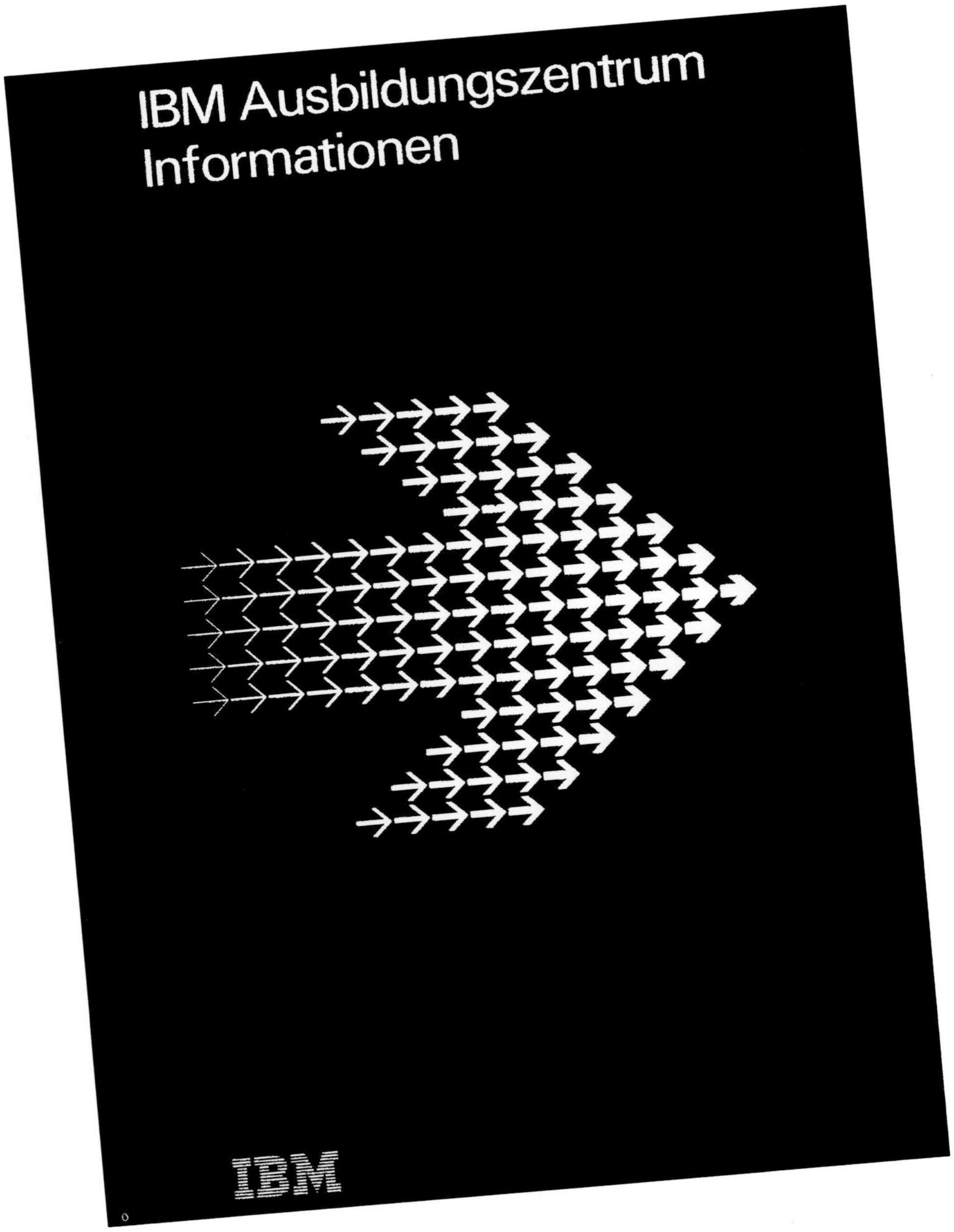

IBM Ausbildungszentrum
Informationen

IBM

The progressively bolder arrows give drama to this jacket cover for an IBM Switzerland report. The jacket is covered almost entirely with black ink, so its "color" comes from the use of reverses to white for the graphic, title, and IBM logo.

Reel Conversations
Book Jacket

DESIGN FIRM
Pentagram Design
(New York, New York)

ART DIRECTOR
Steven Brower / Carol Publishing Group

DESIGNER
Paula Scher / Pentagram Design

CLIENT
Carol Publishing Group

This soft-cover book jacket uses black ink, halftones on a white paper stock, and matte lamination to help it stand out from other books in a bookstore. All type is handlettered.

Healthy People 2000
Brochure

DESIGN FIRM
Mark Oldach Design
(Chicago, Illinois)

ART DIRECTOR
Mark Oldach

PHOTOGRAPHY
Stock

CLIENT
American Hospital Association

Healthy People 2000

America's Hospitals Respond

A resource kit to help you mobilize a community-wide health promotion initiative linked to national Year 2000 objectives.

American Hospital Association

AHA

Bold type and large halftone photographs printed with large-dot screens combine to give this resource kit its bold, eye-catching look. A red-metal spiral binding adds a touch of color. The booklet's objective is to help hospital marketing personnel understand and communicate information about a federal government-sponsored initiative to increase awareness of health concerns by the year 2000.

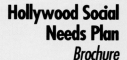

DESIGN FIRM
CRA/LA
(Los Angeles, California)

ART DIRECTOR
Dino Bernardi

CLIENT
Hollywood Redevelopment Project

Mental health services are needed for a range of client groups. Since the completion of the study there has been a further erosion of available Los Angeles County mental health services in the community.

Job training, development, and placement is needed in Hollywood. The average family income in Hollywood is approximately $15,000 (Citywide: $26,000). Jobs and job training are particularly needed for single parent families, immigrants and refugees, youth, minorities, veterans, and homeless.

Short term shelter, transitional housing, and innovative homeless prevention programs are needed to reach those at high risk of homelessness. Indicative of the need for such programs, between October 1987 and September 1988, 1,428 homeless youth were provided shelter while 3,034 were turned away.

The expected increase in non-English speaking immigrants and refugees (mainly Hispanics, Soviet Armenians, and Asian Pacifics) will increase the need for multi-lingual, ethnically oriented social services; English as a second language classes; and job training and placement.

SECTION I.
Policies

The Hollywood Social Needs Plan is, foremost, a commitment to promote existing social service network within the Hollywood Redevelopment Project as a comprehensive system of care, where Agency resources can be used to strengthen the system's abilities, efficacy, and responsiveness in a diverse community during an era of reduced government spending. ◆ This commitment reflects the belief that a coordinated systematic approach to delivering the community's service needs will reduce duplication of services, provide for more efficient programming of services, and will enable area providers to share data and focus on thereby identifying and filling system. ◆ The Plan and local funds community's

HOLLYWOOD SOCIAL NEEDS PLAN

Community
Redevelopment
Agency of the
City of
Los Angeles

Hollywood
Redevelopment
Project

Designer Dino Bernard's original graphic depicts the diverse population and cultural elements that comprise Hollywood, California—an appropriate graphic focal point for this plan outlining a new comprehensive approach to meeting that community's social needs.

Tugomer
Poster and Program Booklet

DESIGN FIRM
KROG
(Ljubljana, Slovenia)

ART DIRECTOR
Edi Berk

PHOTOGRAPHER
Tone Stojko

CLIENT
MGL Ljubljana
(Town Theater of Ljubljana)

Hand-lettered graffiti-style type and a stark, shadow-effect photograph combine to give power and drama to this theater poster and accompanying program booklet. High-contrast halftones throughout the booklet continue the somber effect. "Tugomer," a play by the young Slovenian playwright Vili Ravnjak, is a modern paraphrase of a famous Slovenian myth about a national traitor.

Tomaž Toporišič

"Zorislava ljubi me! Vse mi je še potem mogoče učiniti in popraviti."

TUGOMEROVE METAMORFOZE

JOSIP JURČIČ PROTI KONCU SEDMEGA PRIZORA ZADNJEGA DEJANJA SVOJE ROKOPISNE DRAME, KI BO POSTALA PRVOTNO BESEDILO, NA PODLAGI KATEREGA BODO LEVSTIK KOT SODOBNIK, ZA NJIM PA ŠE OSTALI, IZPISOVALI SVOJE AVTORSKE VARIACIJE *TUGOMEROVE* USODE, V RAZBURJENA USTA SVOJEGA GLAVNEGA JU... ...GORNJE BESEDE. VRH DRAME JE ŽE ZA NAMI, Z BLISKOVITOSTJO SE BLIŽA JUNAKOV VRATOLOMNI KOLAPS... ...K PROTIIGRE... IN VENDAR JE ŽE VSEM JASNO, DA JE NJEGOV ZNAČAJ "MRAČNEGA EROT... ...TON SLODNJAK) VSE PREJ KOT ZAPISAN JURČIČU, TAKO LJUBEMU LJUBEZENS... ... NASVETIH PRIJATELJEV POSTAVIL JUNAKE PRVE SLOVENSKE TRAGEDIJE... ...V TRAGIČNO KONČAL, S SEBOJ PA BO V TRAGEDIJO POTEGNIL TUDI SVOJ NAROD. ■ FRAN LEVSTIK JE S TEM IZ JURČIČEVE MAŠČEVALKA ZORISLAVA, TUGOMEROVA NESOJENA ŽENA IN VDOV... ...ELODRAME, KI JE OB NARODNI TEMATIKI IZPOSTAVLJALA PREDVSEM USODNOST JUNAKOVEGA Z ROMANTIKO SNUBEC, MU BO ŽE V NASLEDNJEM PRIZORU ZABODLA NOŽ V P... ...ČUSTVOVANJA TER GA PRIMERNO ZAČINJEVALA S POGOJNO REALISTIČNIMI DIALOGI IN MONOLO- TRAGEDIJE NA PODLAGI PISANJA NEMŠKEGA ZGODOVINARJA L... ...NDENČNO IN PRECEJ FORMALISTIČNO "TRAGEDIJO" V VERZIH. IZRAZITO ENOSTAVNO IN PRIPELJAN DO KONCA. TAKEGA ALI DRUGAČNEGA. ZA JURČIČE... ...BRO JURČIČEVE "TRAGEDIJE" JE S TEM ZAMENJALA NEPRIMERNO OB- VSEM S STALIŠČA DRAMATURGIJE TRAGEDIJE PRECEJ SPO... ...ŠE VEDNO ZELO FORMALISTIČNA IN OKORNA "TRAGEDIJA" Z ARHAIČNOSTI TUDI NADVSE PRIVLAČNEGA. TAKO ZA LITERA... ...NJENEGA NEGATIVCA, KI JE SPOSOBEN ŠE PRECEJ VEČ JE V KOMENTARJU K LEVSTIKOVEMU *TUGOMERU* VEČ K... ...OD KAKRŠNEGA KOLI NEVARNEGA INDIVIDUALIZMA, JE KOT "SEKSUALNEGA BLAZNIKA IN GERMANSKEGA PO... ...MER CELO FIZIČNO MANJ IMPOZANTEN OD SVOJIH TEKME- ZGODOVINE SLOVENSKEGA NARODA, NEPOPRAV... ...KOT NARODNIH JUNAKOV V SLUŽBI OBČESTVA, KI MU PRI- LJUBEZENSKE BLAZNOSTI ZA DOSEGO SVOJEGA CI... ...BNIKOV PAČ LAHKO FUNKCIONIRAL KOT PARADIGMATIČEN LIK ČELIGOJA, ŽRTVUJE SVOJE PRIJATELJE KARANTAN... ...Č ZGODOVINSKA NUJNOST, KI PA SE BO V NADALJNJEM BOJU ZA ME DEVA ČUTIM. POLJUBI ZADNJIKRA... ...EGA NARODA, MED KATEREGA PREDNIKE GA JE TREBA PRIŠTEVATI. ■

DEJANJA VERZNE VERZIJE *TUGOMERA*, KI JE LETA 1876 POD JURČIČEVIM IMENOM, TODA V MOČNI PREDELAVI AVTORSKE ROKE FRANA LEVSTIKA KONČNO IZŠLA V KNJIŽNI OBLIKI, JE TRAGIČEN KONEC ŠE OČITNEJŠI KOT PRI PRVI JURČIČEVI VERZIJI. TODA GLAVNI JUNAK, Z NJIM PA TUDI ISTOIMENSKA TRAGEDIJA, STA V ENEM LETU, KI LOČI NASTANEK PRVE IN DRUGE VERZIJE, DOŽIVELA NEVERJETNE METAMORFOZE. TUGOMER NE GOVORI VEČ ZORISLAVI, KI JO FATALNO LJUBI, ZARADI TE LJUBEZNI UBIJA, IZDAJA ITD., ONA PA GA PREZIRA. IZDIHNIL BO TAKO REKOČ V ROKAH LJUBLJENE ŽENE, KI MU NAMENJA VSO SVOJO NEŽNOST IN LJUBEZEN. Z EROSOM OBSEDENEGA NEGATIVCA JE ZAMENJAL PREZAUPLJIVI ČLOVEKOLJUB IN IDEALIST, KI BO BREZ KRIVDE

Vili Ravnjak

TUGOMER
ALI TISTI, KI MERI ŽALOST

North Shore Fish
Poster

DESIGN FIRM
Market Sights
(Washington, D.C.)

DESIGNER
Marilyn Worseldine

CLIENT
Studio Theatre

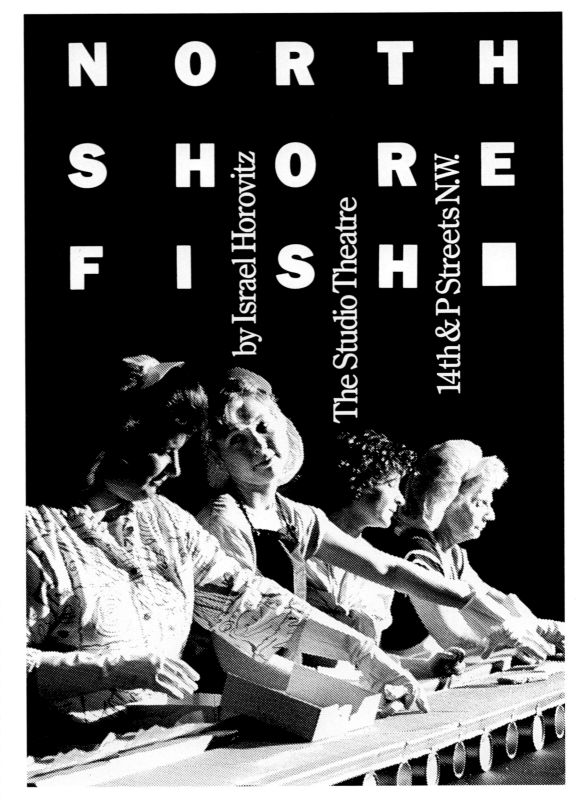

The Studio Theatre is a small repertory theater company with very limited budgets. Posters advertising its productions must always be produced with black ink only. For designer Marilyn Worseldine, this is not a limitation, since stark black and white images help reinforce the gritty urban stage experiences that the Studio offers. For each production, she visualizes a single image to express the play's concept. Originally, Market Sights arranged for the posters to be

The Bacchae
Poster

DESIGN FIRM
Market Sights
(Washington, D.C.)

DESIGNER
Marilyn Worseldine

CLIENT
Studio Theatre

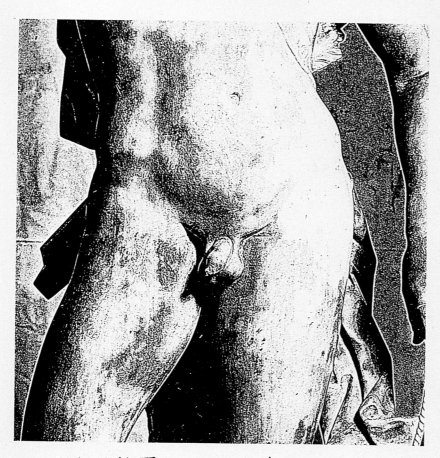

commercially printed. Now, however, the Studio takes advantage of improvements in copy machines and photocopies each design for posting around Washington, D.C.

Jerzy Kosinski:
The Face and Masks
Poster

DESIGN FIRM
Tadeusz Piechura
(Lódź, Poland)

ART DIRECTOR
Tadeusz Piechura

PHOTOGRAPHER
Czeslaw Czaplinski

CLIENT
Muzeum Sztuki-Lódź

A close-up photograph of Jerzy Kosinski seems to questioningly stare out at the observer in this promotional poster for a museum exhibition of Kosinsky's work.

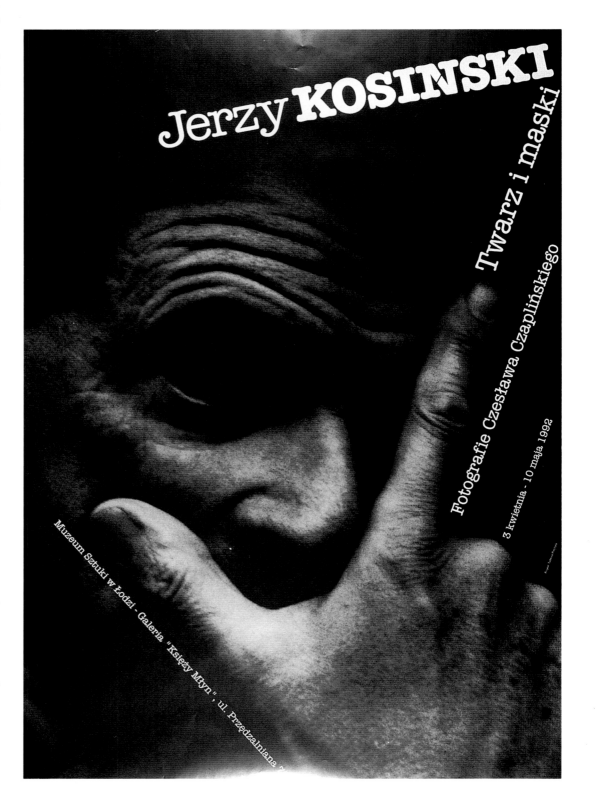

Ntozake Shange's

Exhilarating Choreopoem

S P E L L # 7 :

geechee jibara
quick magic trance
manual for technologically
stressed third world people

Starring Kenneth Daugherty

Ezra Knight

Kelly Taffe

Ron O.J. Parson

Tracie Jade Jenkins

Denise Diggs

"Lovely Cathy Simpson

and powerful" Directed by Bus Howard Choreographed by

-N.Y Times Ron Himes Jewell Robinson Mike Malone

Wednesday-Saturday 8pm
Sunday 2 and 8pm
Tickets $14.50-$22.50

The Studio Theatre

14th and P Streets, NW

202-332-3300

DESIGN FIRM
Market Sights
(Washington, D.C.)

DESIGNER
Marilyn Worseldine

CLIENT
Studio Theatre

As with the posters on pages 26 and 27, designer Marilyn Worseldine prepared this poster—advertising a Japanese drama being staged for a Washington, D.C., repertory theater—using only black ink. The theater then photocopied it for distribution around the city.

Pentagram Club of Stars
Poster

DESIGN FIRM
Pentagram Design
(London, England)

ART DIRECTOR
Alan Fletcher

CLIENT
AIGA Washington

AIGA WASHINGTON PRESENTS **AN EVENING WITH PENTAGRAM** ALAN FLETCHER, KIT HINRICHS, WOODY PIRTLE. 27 FEBRUARY 1990. RECEPTION 6:30 PM. LECTURE 7:30 PM. LOCATION DUPONT PLAZA HOTEL, EMBASSY HALL BALLROOM, 1500 NEW HAMPSHIRE AVENUE, NW, WASHINGTON, DC 20036.

Pentagram Design used an assortment of five-pointed stars to symbolically suggest the studio's name while promoting a lecture by three of the studio's principals for members of the Washington, D.C., chapter of the American Institute of Graphic Arts.

Save San Francisco Bay
Poster

DESIGN FIRM
Akagi Design
(San Francisco, California)

ART DIRECTOR
Doug Akagi

DESIGNERS
Doug Akagi, Kimberly Powell

CLIENT
Akagi Design

Designer Doug Akagi printed his original Gyotaku print of a striped bass on newsprint and then (using an inspiration from his wife) crumpled the paper, suggesting the time-honored practice of wrapping fish in old newspapers. The poster, prepared for an AIGA event in San Francisco, also included text explaining the declining populations of striped bass in San Francisco Bay's delta waters.

New Voices, Sounds and Visuals
Poster

DESIGN FIRM
Niklaus Troxler
(Willisau, Switzerland)

ART DIRECTOR
Niklaus Troxler

CLIENT
Jazz in Willisau

This black-and-white silkscreen poster promoting a concert by a jazz vocal group with a multimedia show uses the hide spots of cows as a subtle graphic pattern.

Werner Lüdi Sunnymoon
Poster

DESIGN FIRM
Niklaus Troxler
(Willisau, Switzerland)

ART DIRECTOR
Niklaus Troxler

CLIENT
Jazz in Willisau

Silhouettes of musicians
playing jazz instruments
combine to give drama to
this silkscreened poster
promoting a big-
band concert.

Paul Davis,
Visiting Artist
Poster

DESIGN FIRM
Michael Fanizza and Cedomir Kostovic
(Norfolk, Virginia)

ART DIRECTOR
Michael Fanizza

DESIGNERS
Michael Fanizza and Cedomir Kostovic

CLIENT
Art Department, Old Dominion
University

Computer drawing and scanning software were used to design this silkscreened poster, which interweaves illustrations with bold sans-serif type and a brief bio of the award-winning graphic designer Paul Davis. This poster was prepared to promote a lecture by Davis at the Fine and Performing Arts Center of Old Dominion University.

Art Department   Paul Davis   Lecture   Old Dominion University

February 18, 1992

7:30pm

Fine & Performing Arts Center

Room 107   Norfolk, Virginia

PAUL DAVIS

Paul Davis, Graphic Designer and Illustrator is the principal of his own design firm *Paul Davis Studio*. He has been one of the world's most influential illustrators and art directors for over thirty years. He was a member of the renowned *Push Pin Studio* with Milton Glaser and Seymour Chwast between 1959 and 1963. Since starting his own studio his work has been published in every major design publication, both in the United States and abroad. His work spans the range of disciplines that fall under the general term graphic design. He has designed and illustrated books including *Bouquet: Twelve Flower Fables* by Myrna Davis, magazines such as *Wig Wag* and *Normal*, and posters for cultural events and social causes. His work has won several Art Director's Club Gold Medals. He is a graduate of the School of Visual Arts where he now teaches. Paul Davis is the 1989 recipient of the AIGA Gold Medal.

Cafe Corina
Packaging

DESIGN FIRM
Market Sights
(Washington, D.C.)

DESIGNER
Marilyn Worseldine

CLIENT
Cafe Corina

Cafe Corina, a small coffee-roasting business, started out being able to afford only a plain black stock bag for packaging its beans. With relatively small quantities of the product being produced, Cafe Corina was ready to add a label by hand and test the market. The one-color label—black with reverse image—visually disappears on the package, making the product look as large as possible on the shelf. The intense, rich black is perfect for the dark-roasted coffee targeted to small gourmet stores in the Washington, D.C., area.

Endangered Animals
Lunch Bags

DESIGN FIRM
Stephanie Milanowski
(Grand Rapids, Michigan)

ART DIRECTOR
Stephanie Milanowski

CLIENT
Stephanie Milanowski / Save Me
Lunch Bags

Each of these nine lunch bags features a specific endangered animal. One side of each bag features an original illustration of the animal, with the other side describing the animal in language a young student can understand—e.g., a Florida manatee is "as long as a row of 20 basketballs."

T W O

Green
346

Yellow
125

COLOR

Périscope
Stationery

DESIGN FIRM
Verge, LeBel Communication
(Québec, Québec, Canada)

ART DIRECTOR
Marie Rodrigue

DESIGNERS
Chantale Audet, Chantal Demers

CLIENT
Théâtre Périscope

A flecked deep-ivory paper and subdued screen of the client's logo on the letterhead and folder give this stationery package a look suggesting more colors than the two actually used. The folder is printed on the same paper stock and weight as the business card, but by covering the folder almost entirely with a deep brown ink, it appears to have been printed on a different paper.

Collins & Chu
Stationery

DESIGN FIRM
Collins & Chu (Tustin, California)

ART DIRECTOR
Collins & Chu

DESIGNER
Lorna Moy-Masaki

ILLUSTRATOR
Johnee Bee

CLIENT
Collins & Chu

With a logo illustration
suggesting the design
studio's staff, this stationery
system simply but effectively
conveys Collins & Chu's
individuality and
personality.

Global Care Products
Stationery

DESIGN FIRM
Turquoise Design
(Hull, Québec, Canada)

ART DIRECTOR
Mark Timmings

DESIGNER
Mario Godbout

CLIENT
Global Care Products

1275 Richmond Road, Unit 1805, Ottawa, Ontario, Canada, K2B 8E3   (613) 828-5468, Fax (613) 828-1181

Effective use of both black and green inks, and of a variable-dot screen in printing the client's globe logo, help make this stationery system successful. The back of the letterhead sheet is printed with the green stripe effect shown above for the address side of the business card — a pattern achieved by alternating solids and screens of the green ink. Also printed on the back of the letterhead is Global Products' corporate mission statement, so that it is the first thing one reads upon opening the envelope.

Brooks Howard
Stationery

DESIGN FIRM
Evenson Design Group
(Culver City, California)

ART DIRECTOR
Stan Evenson

DESIGNERS
Stan Evenson, Glenn Sakamoto

CLIENT
Brooks Howard

As the only element printed
in a color other than black,
the running-man logo
becomes the dominant focus
in this stationery system for
Brooks Howard, a duplicator
of various audio and
video products.

Travel Services
of America
Stationery

DESIGN FIRM
Hornall Anderson Design Works
(Seattle, Washington)

ART DIRECTOR
Jack Anderson

DESIGNERS
Jack Anderson, David Bates,
Julia LaPine, Mary Hermes

ILLUSTRATORS
David Bates, Yutaka Sasaki

CLIENT
Travel Services of America

This stationery system for a travel agency that wanted to project a service-oriented image combines soft blue and brown shades, delicate type, and a cream-colored paper stock. The logo of an airplane superimposed on a globe effectively conveys the nature of the client's business as a travel agency involved in global, rather than only domestic, travel (as the firm's name might suggest).

Aviatic Club
Stationery

DESIGN FIRM
RM Communication Design
(Sainte-Foy, Québec, Canada)

ART DIRECTOR
Julie Létourneau

DESIGNERS
Julie Létourneau, Marie Rodrigue

CLIENT
Aviatic Club

GARE DU PALAIS
SUITE 104
QUÉBEC
G1K 3X2
TÉL.: 418.522.35.55
FAX : 418.522.64.04

The green and red inks used for the letterhead and envelope for the Aviatic Club restaurant/bar are the same, but the use of two different paper colors causes somewhat different effects. Both pieces use screens of the green ink to subtly print sketches of early aviators. The design was intended to express the personality of the Aviatic Club, which is modeled after a men's club of the mid-1940s.

Manlove Photography
Stationery

DESIGN FIRM
Ross Design
(Wilmington, Delaware)

ART DIRECTOR
Tony Ross

ILLUSTRATOR
John Francis

CLIENT
Joe Manlove

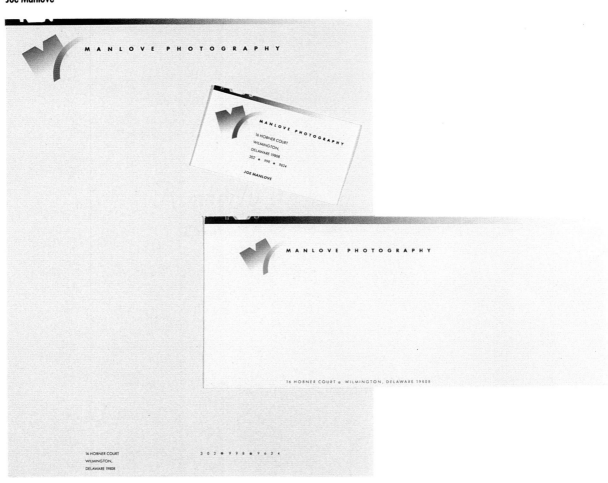

Recognizing that stationery packages are usually printed on different presses, Ross Design used a different second color for each element of this package. The client's photography business is connoted by the film-negative-like notches cut out of the left side of the gradated black strip that flows across the top of each item in the stationery package.

DESIGN FIRM
O&J Design
(New York, New York)

ART DIRECTOR
Andrzej J. Olejniczak

DESIGNERS
Andrzej J. Olejniczak, I. Clara Kim

CLIENT
Andrée Light Options

Yellow rays of light on this stationery convey the client's custom-lighting business. The effect is further enhanced by the screens that are used with the black-ink type and the short strip at the base of each element in the stationery system.

Susie Cushner
Photography
Stationery

DESIGN FIRM
Clifford Selbert Design
(Cambridge, Massachusetts)

ART DIRECTORS
Clifford Selbert, Melanie Lowe

DESIGNER
Melanie Lowe

PHOTOGRAPHER
Susie Cushner

CLIENT
Susie Cushner Photography

By using screened-back
halftones, this stationery not
only conveys the nature of
photographer Susie
Cushner's business; it also
provides samples of the rich
textures and shadows that
are characteristic
of her work.

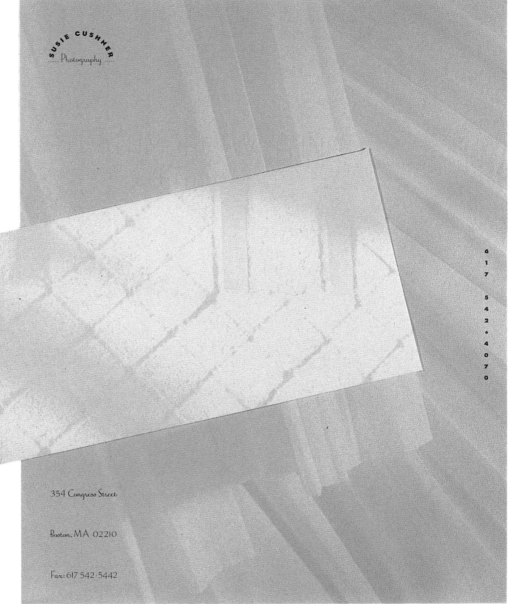

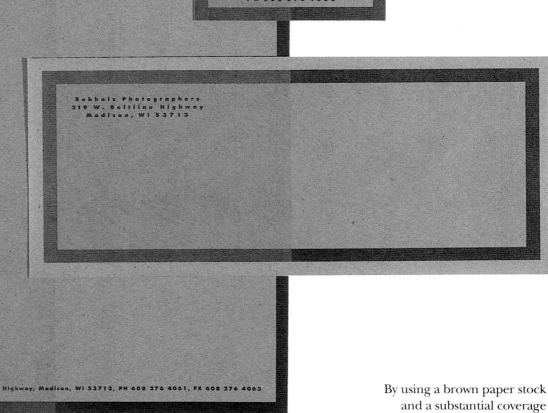

Rebholz Photographers
Stationery

DESIGN FIRM
Planet Design Company
(Madison, Wisconsin)

ART DIRECTOR
Kevin Wade, Dana Lytle

DESIGNERS
Kevin Wade, Tom Jenkins

CLIENT
Rebholz Photographers

By using a brown paper stock and a substantial coverage with a light screen of the black ink, Planet Design Company produced a stationery system for Rebholz Photographers that suggests four colors, even though it is printed using only two inks.

Bud Lammers
Stationery

DESIGN FIRM
Collins & Chu
(Tustin, California)

ART DIRECTORS
Bill Collins, Cynthia Zech-Rhodes

CLIENT
Bud Lammers

Bold black and red inks on an ivory paper stock combine with a distinctive display typeface and bold highlighting of the client's first name to give this stationery system its attractive look.

Dance Umbrella of Ontario
Stationery

DESIGN FIRM
Telmet Design Associates
(Toronto, Ontario, Canada)

ART DIRECTOR
Tiit Telmet

DESIGNERS
Joseph Gault, Tiit Telmet

CLIENT
Dance Umbrella of Ontario

Telmet Design Associates created a logo conveying movement and change in a theatrical setting as the central element of this stationery system. The nonprofit Dance Umbrella of Ontario provides administrative services to independent choreographers in Ontario.

Rhombus
Stationery

DESIGN FIRM
Telmet Design Associates
(Toronto, Ontario, Canada)

ART DIRECTOR
Tiit Telmet

DESIGNERS
Joseph Gault, Charles Reynolds

CLIENT
Rhombus Development Corporation

By overprinting blue and yellow inks to produce the greenish black strip across the top of this letterhead and envelope, Telmet Design Associates produced a three-color effect on a two-color press. Precise registration of this overprint proved to be a production challenge, as did trimming off the letterhead's upper right-hand corner.

Sukowicz, Lenich & Company
Stationery

DESIGN FIRM
JOED Design
(Chicago, Illinois)

ART DIRECTOR
Edward Rebek

CLIENT
Sukowicz, Lenich & Company

Sukowicz, Lenich & Company
CERTIFIED PUBLIC ACCOUNTANTS

J. RUSSELL LENICH, CPA
PARTNER

Sukowicz, Lenich & Company
CERTIFIED PUBLIC ACCOUNTANTS

110 E. SCHILLER STREET, SUITE 318, ELMHURST, IL 60126
PHONE 708.782.2000 / FAX 708.782.2002

Sukowicz, Lenich & Company
CERTIFIED PUBLIC ACCOUNTANTS

110 E. SCHILLER STREET, SUITE 318, ELMHURST, IL 60126

110 E. SCHILLER STREET, SUITE 318, ELMHURST, IL 60126 / PHONE 708.782.2000 / FAX 708.782.2002

This stationery system for a firm of certified public accountants is intended to project not only professionalism, reliability, and honesty—but also creativity and a way of making all the numbers line up straight. The slate blue and gray inks combine for a contemporary yet conservative elegance.

Cafe Toma
Stationery

DESIGN FIRM
Bruce Yelaska Design
(San Francisco, California)

ART DIRECTOR
Bruce Yelaska

CLIENT
Cafe Toma

Designer Bruce Telaska gave this stationery system an angular look by sloping the logo and text copy and by printing the letterhead and business card on non-traditionally cut paper. Yelaska designed this stationery to reflect the fun and casual nature of Cafe Toma's environment.

Du Verre Glass Limited, 280 Queen St. West, Toronto, Ontario, Canada, M5V 2A1
Telephone 416 593 0182

Du Verre
Stationery

DESIGN FIRM
Concrete Design Communications
(Toronto, Ontario, Canada)

ART DIRECTORS
Diti Katona, John Pylypczak

DESIGNER
Diti Katona

PHOTOGRAPHER
Chris Nicholls

CLIENT
Du Verre Glass Limited

This stationery system's
subdued green illustration of
a plate and fork effectively
conveys Du Verre's
business as a glass and
fine housewares retailer,
while the script type
connotes upscale elegance.

Andrea Klausner
Stationery

DESIGN FIRM
Andrea Klausner
(Vienna, Austria)

ART DIRECTOR
Andrea Klausner

CLIENT
Andrea Klausner

Andrea produced this restrained but distinctive stationery for self-promotion by overprinting black on a purple-gray ink and by dropping out the words "Grafik Design" to appear white.

Pilialoha
Stationery

DESIGN FIRM
Remington Design
(San Francisco, California)

ART DIRECTOR
Dorothy Remington

DESIGNERS
Amelie von Fluegge, Jill Weed

CLIENT
Machiko Heyde

Subtle green prints used as a full-bleed base give a Hawaiian feel to this stationery for a Maui bed-and-breakfast cottage.

Kan Tai-keung
Stationery

DESIGN FIRM
Kan Tai-keung Design & Associates
(Hong Kong)

ART DIRECTOR
Kan Tai-keung

CLIENT
Kan Tai-keung

Designer Kan Tai-keung blends contemporary graphic form with Chinese ink painting in this stationery system. The result is a demonstration of his skills both as a graphic artist and as an illustrator. Extra color was added by selecting different shades of blue for the two pieces.

Raymond Bellemare
Stationery

DESIGN FIRM
Raymond Bellemare Designers
(Noyan, Québec, Canada)

ART DIRECTOR
Raymond Bellemare

CLIENT
Raymond Bellemare Designers

RAYMOND BELLEMARE
703, ROUTE 225
NOYAN, QUÉBEC, CANADA J0J 1B0
(514) 294 2612

Bright red dots printed on the back side of this letterhead peek through the paper stock to produce a subdued pink base. This pattern provides a nice complement to the green and red type and apple-tree logo on the letterhead's front, though registration proved challenging. The red dots are also used on the back of the business card but do not show through the cover-weight stock. The logo symbolizes the trees that are part of the country environment around designer Raymond Bellemare's house/studio.

Hummingbird
Stationery

DESIGN FIRM
Meredith Mustard, Art & Design
(Berkeley, California)

ART DIRECTOR
Judy Tollefson

DESIGNERS
Judy Tollefson, Meredith Mustard

ILLUSTRATOR / CALLIGRAPHER
Meredith Mustard

CLIENT
Hummingbird Associates

A beautifully drawn hummingbird effectively suggests the name of the orthodontic-consulting business for which this stationery system was designed. The chief challenge in producing this letterhead was calculating the screen values of the light purple and blue-gray inks so that they were similar enough to allow a readable letter to be typed over the final image.

Ellen Cassidy
Stationery

DESIGN FIRM
Ellen Cassidy
(Springfield, Pennsylvania)

ART DIRECTOR
Ellen Cassidy

CLIENT
Ellen Cassidy

Ellen Cassidy's chief
challenge in producing
personal stationery was in
creating a package that
would promote her as both
an illustrator and a designer.
Her crisp graphic works
well with the fine rules
and delicate type.

François Côté Collection
Stationery

DESIGN FIRM
RM Communication Design
(Sainte-Foy, Québec, Canada)

ART DIRECTOR
Marie Rodrigue

CLIENT
François Côté Collection

The François Côté Collection is given an upscale image with this letterhead featuring the menswear store's name as a black signature, atop a large, sloped shadow of the signature produced with a separate gray ink. The formal appearance is enhanced with a moiré-pattern on the envelope flap and the back of the letterhead and card.

Icon Acoustics
Stationery

DESIGN FIRM
Clifford Selbert Design
(Cambridge, Massachusetts)

ART DIRECTORS
Clifford Selbert, Lynn Riddle Waller

DESIGNERS
Lynn Riddle Waller

CLIENT
Icon Acoustics

Use of different papers, including an elephant-hide-pattern stock for the letterhead and business card, gives this two-color stationery system a four-color appearance. The logo subtly alludes to the celestial names of the company's loudspeakers.

Cue
Stationery

DESIGN FIRM
Annette Harcus Design
(Double Bay, New South Wales, Australia)

ART DIRECTOR
Annette Harcus

DESIGNER
Stephanie Martin

CLIENT
Cue Clothing Company

Cue Clothing is a national manufacturer and retailer of women's fashion in Australia that has been in business since the 1960s. The graphic identity for the company had to portray fashion style with a sense of history. Annette Harcus Design was given a two-color restriction for its work because of the numerous and varied stationery and form applications involved with the project.

DESIGN FIRM
Pentagram Design
(San Francisco, California)

ART DIRECTOR
Kit Hinrichs

DESIGNER
Catherine Wong

CLIENT
Hirasuna Editorial

HIRASUNA EDITORIAL

DELPHINE HIRASUNA

901 BATTERY STREET
SUITE 212
SAN FRANCISCO, CA 94111
TEL. 415.986.8014
FAX. 415.986.7649

HIRASUNA EDITORIAL
901 BATTERY STREET
SUITE 212
SAN FRANCISCO, CA 94111

901 BATTERY STREET
SUITE 212
SAN FRANCISCO, CA 94111
TEL. 415.986.8014
FAX. 415.986.7649

A brown, serif "H" with a gray, script-letter shadow provides a sophisticated logo for a San Francisco editorial-writing business. Because of the fine lines of the design, the stationery had to be lithographed instead of engraved, as was originally planned.

Italia
Identity

DESIGN FIRM
Hornall Anderson Design Works
(Seattle, Washington)

ART DIRECTOR
Jack Anderson

DESIGNERS
Jack Anderson, Julia LaPine

ILLUSTRATOR
Julia LaPine

CLIENT
Italia

Despite their many-colored appearance, these promotional items for an Italian restaurant, deli, and bakery were all produced using a two-color press. A split-fountain was used with the second color, enabling multiple inks to be inserted into one fountain of the press, then sprayed at random onto the item being printed. The varied graphics used on each element of the identity package illustrate the diversity of Italia's services and products.

Manfred Gallery
Identity

DESIGN FIRM
Rushton Green and Grossutti
(Toronto, Ontario, Canada)

ART DIRECTORS
Keith Rushton, Marcello Grossutti

DESIGNER
Kirsti Ronback

CLIENT
Manfred Gallery

The earthy tints of recycled paper (for stationery and business cards) and kraft paper (for bags and packaging) give extra color to the printed materials designed by Rushton Green and Grossutti. The client, Manfred Gallery, exhibits and sells arts and crafts.

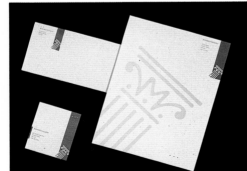

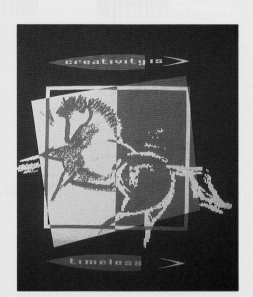

Cowell Design
Promotional T-Shirt

DESIGN FIRM
Cowell Design Group
(Burbank, California)

CREATIVE DIRECTOR
Lee Cowell

ART DIRECTOR
Kevin Weinman

DESIGNER
Anthoney C. Sweeney

CLIENT
Cowell Design Group

Cowell Design Group designed this T-shirt, used by the studio as a holiday giveaway, entirely on a computer. Designs for the front and back were output as film separations directly to the printer via a modem. The purple and yellow horse graphic, printed on the back of the shirt, was created specifically for this promotion. The front of the shirt (not shown here) displayed the studio's logo/name.

TEMPO Madison
10th Anniversary Invitation and Program

DESIGN FIRM
Detter Graphic Design
(Madison, Wisconsin)

ART DIRECTOR
Jeanne Detter

DESIGNER
Jane Nass Barnidge

WRITER
Jenifer Winiger

CLIENT
TEMPO Madison

This invitation and program for the 10th anniversary celebration of a Madison organization of professional women incorporated the logo of *Mirabella* magazine to help draw attention to the event's guest speaker, publisher Grade Mirabella. Detter Graphic Design's choice of inks and paper stocks helped give both pieces a formal look while staying within the client's limited budget.

TriMark Furniture
Promotion

DESIGN FIRM
Schowalter Design
(Short Hills, New Jersey)

ART DIRECTOR
Toni Schowalter

CLIENT
TriMark Furniture Company

A uniform design and the same black and brown inks give a consistent identity to this packet promoting a contemporary furniture store. Each item of furniture is printed on a separate card so that interior designers can hang them up to look at while designing specific projects, and so that the card can also serve as a self-mailer. The descriptive material follows the design grid used for the mailing packet, which is given a three-color look by its textured green paper.

LeClerc
Birth Announcement

DESIGN FIRM
LeClerc Communications
(West Hills, California)

ART DIRECTOR
Tom LeClerc

CLIENT
Baby LeClerc

This birth announcement features a long accordion-fold sheet using halftone photographs to give the vital details, accompanied by pop-up building blocks spelling out the newborn's name. The announcement is printed on coated white paper with black and purple inks. To save money, each building block was handstamped on different colored stocks.

Roosevelt
Invitation

DESIGN FIRM
New Idea Design
(Omaha, Nebraska)

ART DIRECTOR
Ron Boldt

CLIENT
Western Heritage Museum

When New Idea Design was asked to design an invitation and reply card for a party commemorating the 80th anniversary of President Theodore Roosevelt's visit to Omaha, the sponsoring museum gave the studio copy, a two-color limit, and 10 days to prepare everything and have it in the mail. Art director Ron Boldts decided to use a stylized rendition of Roosevelt's very recognizable face and his signature as the central graphic elements. To further catch the viewer's eye, Boldt used two metallic inks on a cream-colored paper and featured no copy (other than the signature) on the invitation cover.

Candiee and Yiu Kwa
Wedding Invitation

DESIGN FIRM
Kan Tai-keung Design & Associates
(Hong Kong)

ART DIRECTOR
Kan Tai-keung

CLIENT
Candiee and Yiu Kwa

This ornate wedding invitation was printed on a fan inserted into a folder. Although two colors of ink were used—black for the Chinese characters and red for the traditional-style illustration—the brown paper stock gave the piece an attractive three-color look. The verse on the fan served as a greeting to the new couple.

Ana Gabriela
Welcoming Invitation

DESIGN FIRM
Rossana S. Hodoyan
(Tijuana, Baja California, México)

ART DIRECTOR
Rossana S. Hodoyan

CLIENT
Rosalina S. Hodoyan

In addition to using blue and gold inks, this invitation to a private party welcoming a visitor from the interior of Mexico to the Baja coast was printed using thermo heating to give an outstanding shine and texture to the sun.

Bremmer & Goris
Halloween Party Invitation

DESIGN FIRM
Uncommon Design
(Laurel, Maryland)
*submitting for Bremmer & Goris
Communications*

ART DIRECTOR
Dennis Goris

DESIGNERS
Carla Conway, Camilia Copozzi

CLIENT
Bremmer & Goris Communications

Yellow paper stock served as an important complement to the two ink colors of this eerie Halloween party invitation. Thermography was used to give texture to the front side of this oversized postcard.

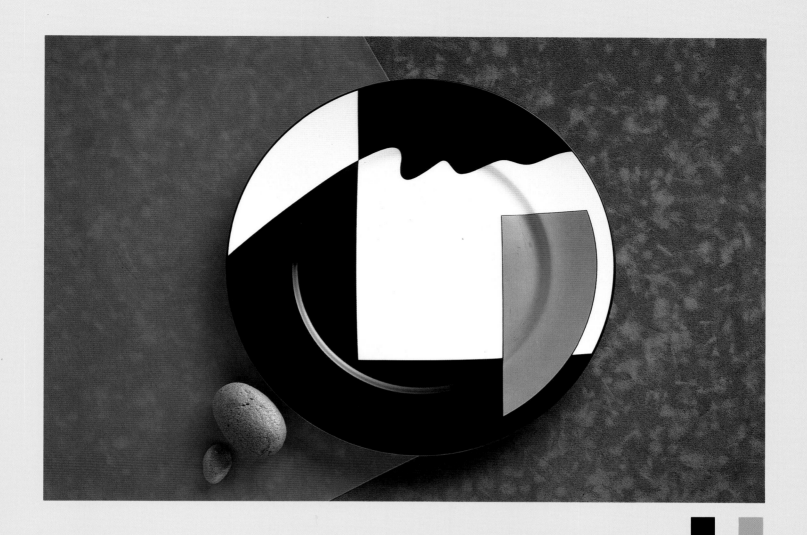

Mikuni
Tableware

DESIGN FIRM
Douglas Design Office
(Tokyo, Japan)

ART DIRECTOR
Douglas Doolittle

PHOTOGRAPHER
Mizukushi Toshimasa

MANUFACTURER
Noritake

CLIENT
Hôtel de Mikuni

Designer Douglas Doolittle
designed this bright and
graphic display plate for a
French restaurant in Japan.
The design evolved from
a variation on the
restaurant's logo.

Bicycle
Shipping Carton

DESIGN FIRM
Visual Marketing Associates
(Dayton, Ohio)

ART DIRECTOR
Kenneth Botts

DESIGNERS
John Walker, Brian Pesti, Kent Miller

CLIENT
Huffy Bicycle Company

Huffy Bicycle Company commissioned Visual Marketing Associates to design a shipping carton for its 16-inch sidewalk bike that could double as a point-of-sale carton. Descriptions of the bike's features are incorporated into the central graphic, with other important information printed down the right margin.

Cicero
Album Cover

DESIGN FIRM
Pentagram Design
(London, England)

ART DIRECTOR / PARTNER
David Hillman

DESIGNERS
David Hillman, Mark Noad

CLIENT
Spaghetti Recordings

Spaghetti Recordings is a small record label started by Tennant & Lowe of the Pet Shop Boys. This cover was prepared for an album by a new singer on the label. The use of two ink colors and an elegant typeface on a white base adds a distinguished air to the cover.

Store your belongings.

STEP
Reebok

Step Reebok
Safety Signs

DESIGN FIRM
The Mednick Group
(Culver City, California)

ART DIRECTORS
Loid Der, Scott Mednick, Cheryl Ruddick

DESIGNER
Loid Der

PHOTOGRAPHER
William Hawkes

CLIENT
Reebok International

"Park Your Stuff" and "Know Your Cruising Speed" were designed to function as part of a series of wall-mounted, health-club signs to be observed during Step Reebok step-training classes. Text and imagery were combined to reinforce the intense, hardcore nature of the exercise itself. Because the signs had to be quite durable, silkscreening was used to print the metallic copper, halftoned imagery, and black typography onto a styrene material.

Joiner Software
Posters

DESIGN FIRM
Planet Design Company
(Madison, Wisconsin)

ART DIRECTORS
Dana Lytle, Kevin Wade

DESIGNER
Dana Lytle

CLIENT
Joiner Software

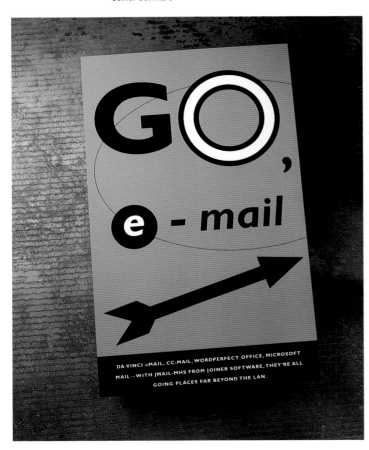

Planet Design Company developed these coordinated posters for Joiner Software for use with an already-existing trade show booth. The booth was all gray, so the posters needed to be colorful to draw attention. The graphics artistically suggest the abilities of Joiner's products at computer performance and networking. Because only three copies of each poster were needed, they were printed by silkscreening.

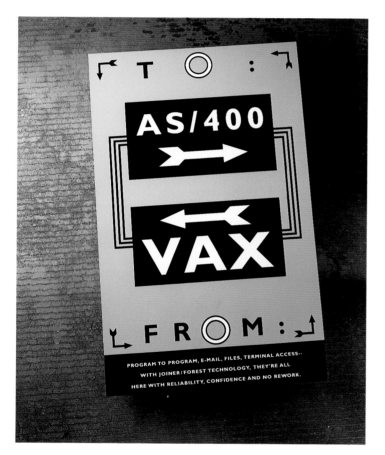

PROGRAM TO PROGRAM, E-MAIL, FILES, TERMINAL ACCESS--
WITH JOINER/FOREST TECHNOLOGY, THEY'RE ALL
HERE WITH RELIABILITY, CONFIDENCE AND NO REWORK.

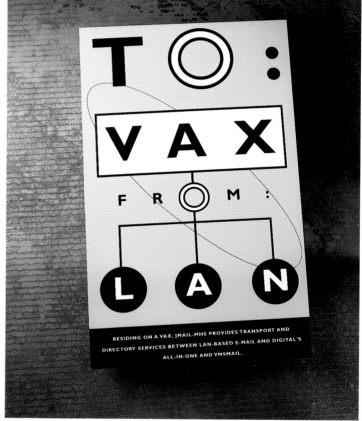

RESIDING ON A VAX, JMAIL-MHS PROVIDES TRANSPORT AND
DIRECTORY SERVICES BETWEEN LAN-BASED E-MAIL AND DIGITAL'S
ALL-IN-ONE AND VMSMAIL.

The XLIth International Art Exhibition of the Venice Biennale 1990
Posters

DESIGN FIRM
Kijuro Yahagi Company
(Tokyo, Japan)

ART DIRECTOR
Kijuro Yahagi

CLIENT
The Japan Foundation for Culture

Designer Kijuro Yahagi used red and white, the colors of the Japanese flag, to provide graphic excitement for these photographic posters promoting Japanese art at an international exhibition in Venice, Italy.

La Biennale di Venezia/XLIV Esposizione Internazionale d'Arte 1990
The XLIVth International Art Exhibition of the Venice Biennale 1990

ENDO Toshikatsu

27 maggio – 30 settembre 1990   May 27 – September 30, 1990

Padiglione Giapponese, Giardini di Castello   Presentato dalla Japan Foundation   Japanese Pavilion, Giardini di Castello   Presented by the Japan Foundation

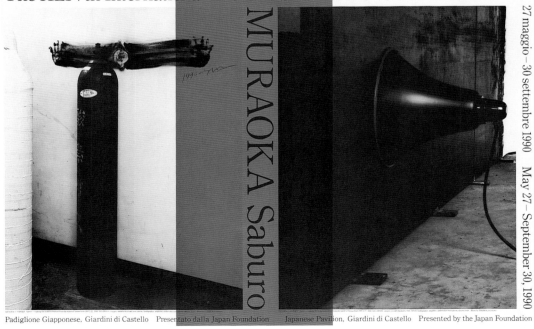

La Biennale di Venezia/XLIV Esposizione Internazionale d'Arte 1990
The XLIVth International Art Exhibition of the Venice Biennale 1990

MURAOKA Saburo

27 maggio – 30 settembre 1990   May 27 – September 30, 1990

Padiglione Giapponese, Giardini di Castello   Presentato dalla Japan Foundation   Japanese Pavilion, Giardini di Castello   Presented by the Japan Foundation

All British Field Meet
Poster

DESIGN FIRM
Hornall Anderson Design Works
(Seattle, Washington)

ART DIRECTOR
Jack Anderson

DESIGNERS
Jack Anderson, David Bates

CLIENT
All British Field Meet

Black and green inks help give an art-deco look to this poster promoting an exhibition of British cars. After this poster was printed on a two-color press, an embossed gold seal was handstamped, in effect adding a subtle but distinctive third color.

Croatia
Poster

DESIGN FIRM
Studio International
(Zagreb, Croatia)

ART DIRECTOR
Boris Ljubičić

CLIENT
Ministry of Information, Republic
of Croatia

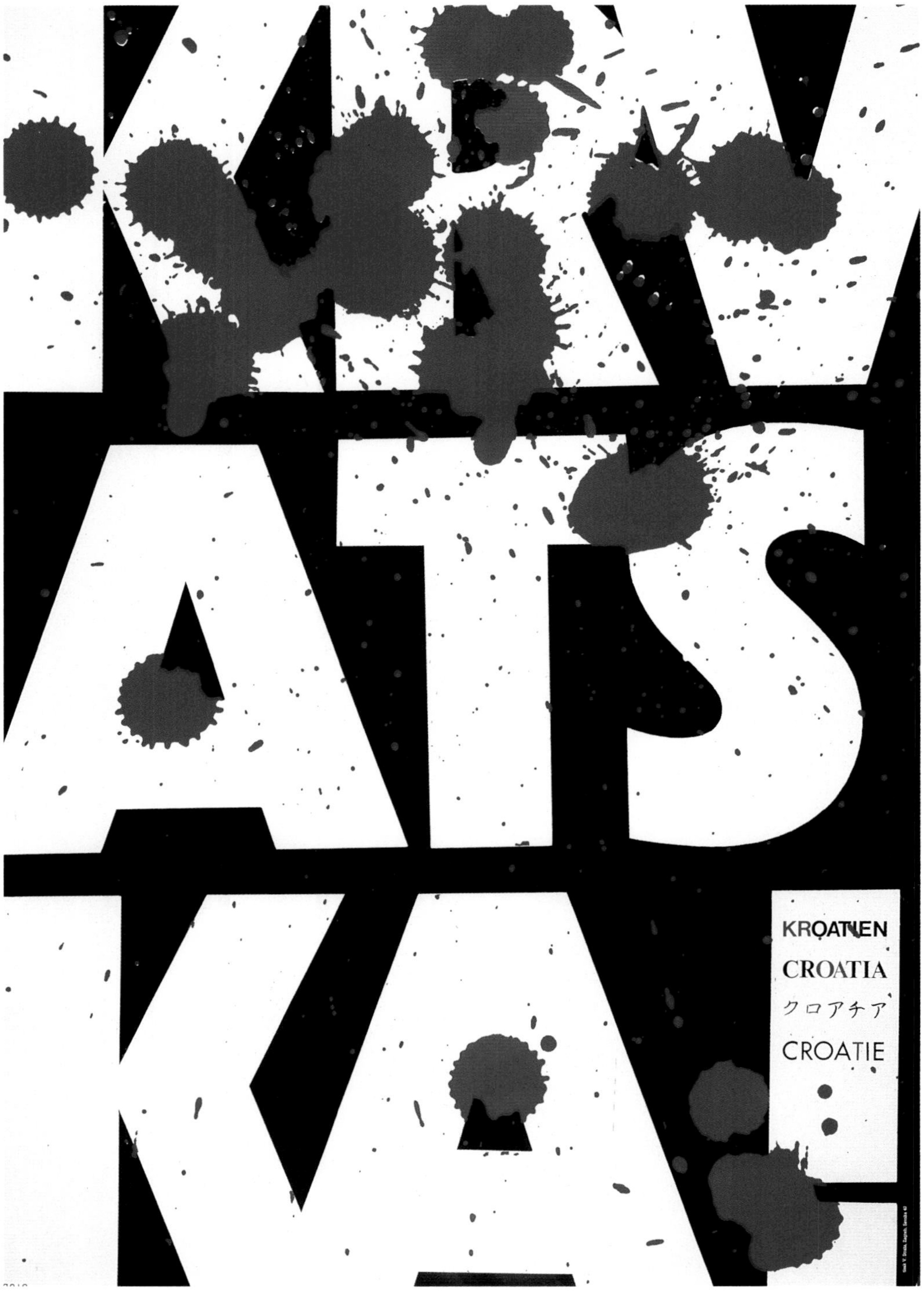

The blood-red ink splattered on bold white type (produced by dropping the text out of a black ink base) give appropriate drama to the poster produced for the new Croatian government to commemorate that county's recent independence movement and war.

KROATIEN

CROATIA

クロアチア

CROATIE

Rage
Poster

DESIGN FIRM
Geneva Design
(Boston, Massachusetts)

ART DIRECTOR
Marc A. Sawyer

ILLUSTRATOR
Linda Bryant

CLIENT
Joan and Robert Parker /
Pearl Productions

WRITTEN BY
JOAN H. PARKER & ROBERT B. PARKER

ADAPTED FOR THE STAGE
From the novel by STEPHEN KING

PRODUCED BY
THE BLACKBURN THEATER COMPANY
& PEARL PRODUCTIONS, INC.

PERFORMED BY
THE ROAD ENSEMBLE

DIRECTED BY
DAN HURLIN

PERFORMING AT THE
BLACKBURN THEATER
MARCH 30, 31 APRIL 1, 2, 6, 7, 9
CURTAIN 8:00 PM
SUNDAYS 5:00 PM

TICKETS AVAILABLE FROM BOSTIX,
THE BLACKBURN THEATER COMPANY
8 ELM STREET, GLOUCESTER, MA 01930
OR CHARGE BY PHONE
(508) 283-9410

A gray handgun pointing
down at red credits and a
blood stain make this poster
a compelling promotion of
a one-act drama in which
a student holds his
classroom hostage.

Mall Poster Campaign
Posters

DESIGN FIRM
Smart Design
(Salt Lake City, Utah)

ART DIRECTOR
Kim Remington

DESIGNER
Craig Reynolds

CLIENT
Smart Design

These posters were prepared for a catalogue that Smart Design created and distributed to shopping malls. Merchants in the malls could then print promotions or announcements on them. Each poster was first silkscreened with a split fountain for the gradated two–color effect, then silkscreened again with gold ink.

VIIIth Mediterranean Games, Split 1979
Poster

DESIGN FIRM
Studio International
(Zagreb, Croatia)

ART DIRECTOR
Boris Ljubičić

CLIENT
Directorate of the VIII Mediterranean
Games, Split 1979

The gradated screening of two shades of blue ink on this poster, with the logo of the Mediterranean Games reversed out in white, successfully suggests rays of light reflecting on a body of water at night. This graphically evokes the picturesque beauty of the Adriatic Sea, on which the games were held.

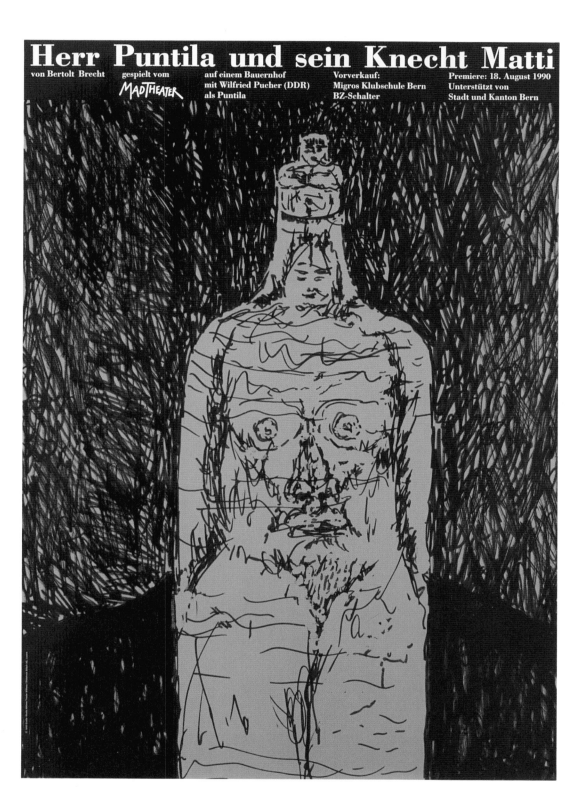

Herr Puntila und sein Knecht Matti
von Bertolt Brecht | gespielt vom **MADTHEATER** | auf einem Bauernhof mit Wilfried Pucher (DDR) als Puntila | Vorverkauf: Migros Klubschule Bern BZ-Schalter | Premiere: 18. August 1990 Unterstützt von Stadt und Kanton Bern

Herr Pentila und Sein Knecht Matti
Poster

DESIGN FIRM
Niklaus Troxler
(Willisau, Switzerland)

ART DIRECTOR
Niklaus Troxler

CLIENT
Mad Theater

Two shades of blue ink and reversed-out white type were used by designer Niklaus Troxler for this promotional poster for a Bern theater company's presentation of a Bertolt Brecht drama.

AIDS Awareness
Poster

DESIGN FIRM
Planet Design Company
(Madison, Wisconsin)

ART DIRECTORS
Kevin Wade, Dana Lytle

DESIGNERS
Erik Johnson, Dana Lytle, Kevin Wade,
Tom Jenkins

ILLUSTRATOR
Erik Johnson

HAND LETTERING
Kevin Wade

CLIENT
Madison AIDS Support Network

Designed as both a thank-you gift for volunteers at the Madison AIDS Support Network and as a promotional tool, this poster was produced by silkscreening two colors onto inexpensive tagboard, with the tagboard used as a third color. The style of illustration and composition, as well as the poster's title, were intended to convey the support group's strength and struggle to overcome AIDS. Planet Design produced 250 copies of this poster while staying within a total budget of $250.

Jazz Festival Willisau '91
Poster

DESIGN FIRM
Niklaus Troxler
(Willisau, Switzerland)

ART DIRECTOR
Niklaus Troxler

CLIENT
Jazz in Willisau

A brush-stroke saxophonist gives eye-catching movement to this silkscreened poster promoting an international jazz festival. The green ink used for the poster's text provides a delicate second color.

Bunky Green Quartet
Poster

DESIGN FIRM
Niklaus Troxler
(Willisau, Switzerland)

ART DIRECTOR
Niklaus Troxler

CLIENT
Jazz in Willisau

This bold blue-and-green silkscreened poster for a jazz concert features a stylized illustration cleverly blending a full profile of a saxophonist with a face profile of a musician with the mouthpiece of his wind instrument.

Willisau Sa. 1. Dez. '90 20 Uhr Mohren   BUNKY GREEN QUARTET

Seattle Camerata
Poster

DESIGN FIRM
Hornall Anderson Design Works
(Seattle, Washington)

ART DIRECTOR
Jack Anderson

DESIGNERS
Jack Anderson, David Bates,
Julia LaPine

ILLUSTRATOR
David Bates

CLIENT
Seattle Camerata

Split-fountain printing enabled this multicolored poster to be printed on a two-color press. One ink well of the printing press was filled with three colors of ink for the type and central graphic, while a second well contained two inks for the calligraphic background swirls. A flecked paper stock gave added texture to this poster.

Mark Mock
Valentine Party
Poster

DESIGN FIRM
Mark Mock Design Associates
(Denver, Colorado)

ART DIRECTOR
Mark Mock

DESIGNER
Jennifer Gilliland

CLIENT
Mark Mock Design Associates

Effective use of black
reversing to white and
screens of the raspberry
color combine to make this
poster / invitation
entertaining as well as
informing. The UV Ultra II
transparent paper is the
same stock used by Mark
Mock Design Associates for
their business card.

Mark Mock Design Associates, Inc.'s

12th Annual Valentine's Celebration

Party will be held at Brio

Located in Prudential Plaza

1050 17th St., just off the 16th St. Mall

February 13th, 4:30 p.m.– 7:30 p.m.

Gourmet coffee, wine and great goodies

RSVP by February 7, at 292-0801

Entertainment by The Diners

Stage 2 Season
Poster

DESIGN FIRM
Modern Dog
(Seattle, Washington)

ART DIRECTOR
Rich Gerdes / Seattle Repertory
Theatre

DESIGNERS
Michael Strassburger, Robynne Raye

CLIENT
Seattle Repertory Theatre

This poster needed to leave a lasting impression and, at the same time, advertise three different plays over several months. Half of the 500 posters were cut down the vertical black bar so that the upside-down man sometimes appeared right-side up. This essentially created three posters in one.

Parham-Santana
Moving Announcement

DESIGN FIRM
Parham-Santana
(New York, New York)

ART DIRECTOR
John Parham

DESIGNER
Maruchi Santana

CLIENT
Parham-Santana

Parham-Santana's moving announcement was intended to get its message out in a way that would communicate the excitement of the new location. Based on the look of street "sale" flyers, the message was loud and clear; some people actually sent flowers in response. The announcement was silkscreened with opaque white and blue inks on a metallic gold stock. All type was found, handwritten, or computer-generated.

SEATTLE'S MIDWINTER

CELEBRATION OF ARTISTS

FEBRUARY 4 - 15, 1988

For a Artstorm

schedule call

the Downtown Seattle

Association.

623-0340

Artstorm is

a celebration of artists.

It's a chance to meet artists,

view their work, see the latest

in fine art, corporate art collections,

galleries, and architechture.

Nearly 200 free events in all.

Artstorm
Poster

DESIGN FIRM
Hornall Anderson Design Works
(Seattle, Washington)

ART DIRECTOR
Jack Anderson

DESIGNERS
Jack Anderson, David Bates

ILLUSTRATORS
Jack Anderson, Bruce Hale

CLIENT
Downtown Seattle Association

With a fountain filled with
black ink, the second
fountain of the printing press
used for this poster was split
and filled with five inks to
produce this multicolored
poster. The "rips" at the top
and bottom of the poster
were handcut.

Piccadilly Square
Dance Party Ad

DESIGN FIRM
Garth DeCew Group
(Los Angeles, California)

CREATIVE DIRECTOR
Garth F. DeCew

ART DIRECTOR
J. Robert Faulkner

CLIENT
Piccadilly Square

By being the only element in a color other than black, the red face profile provides a bold focal point for this advertisement for a youth-oriented shopping center. The viewer's eye is immediately drawn to the descriptive text flowing from the profile's mouth.

Piccadilly Square
Sale Ad

DESIGN FIRM
Garth DeCew Group
(Los Angeles, California)

CREATIVE DIRECTOR
Garth F. DeCew

ART DIRECTOR
J. Robert Faulkner

CLIENT
Piccadilly Square

An upside-down green alien makes this advertisement an immediate eye-catcher. In addition to the descriptive text wrapping around part of the alien's face, an invitation to an aerobic dancing performance is transmitted between the alien's antennas.

Winterfest
Poster

DESIGN FIRM
Gotham City Graphics
(Burlington, Vermont)

ART DIRECTORS
Stephanie Salmon, Amey Radcliffe

CLIENT
Burlington City Arts

Screens of blue and purple inks, combined with reversed-out snowflakes, give variety to this poster promoting a festival sponsored by Burlington, Vermont's city arts council. The town-scene snow globe gives the poster an added sense of movement.

Seymour Chwast
Lights Up at Tyler!
Poster

DESIGN FIRM
Frank Baseman Graphic Design /
Tyler Design Workshop
(Brooklyn, New York)

ART DIRECTOR
Frank Baseman

CLIENTS
Temple University Tyler School of Art,
Graphic Design Department;
AIGA / Philadelphia

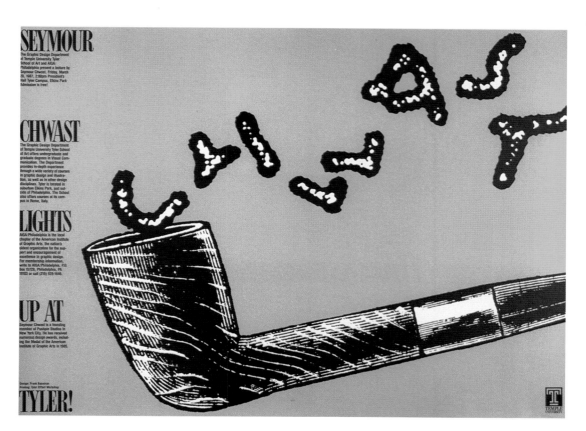

Bold yellow ink provides an eye-catching base for this bright poster announcing a lecture by graphic artist Seymour Chwast. Reverses in the pipe and emerging smoke reveal the actual white color of the paper. The puffs of smoke graphically spell the speaking artist's name.

The Key to Record Storage!
Brochure

DESIGN FIRM
Earl Gee Design
(San Francisco, California)

ART DIRECTOR
Earl Gee

PHOTOGRAPHER
Bill Delzell

CLIENT
Off-Site Record Management

A bold use of yellow, prominent computer-generated graphics, and an unusually large size (11" x 17") combine to help this promotional brochure convey the depth of Off-Site Record Management's services in a way that is hard to ignore.

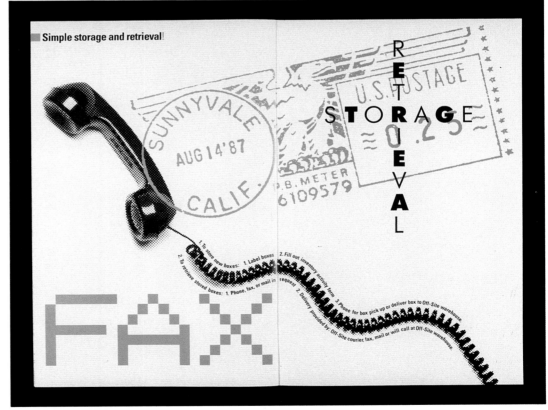

Architecture and Design Forum 2
Newsletter

DESIGN FIRM
Pentagram Design
(San Francisco, California)

ART DIRECTOR
Linda Hinrichs

DESIGNER
Mark T. Selfe

CLIENT
Architecture and Design Forum,
San Francisco Museum of Modern Art

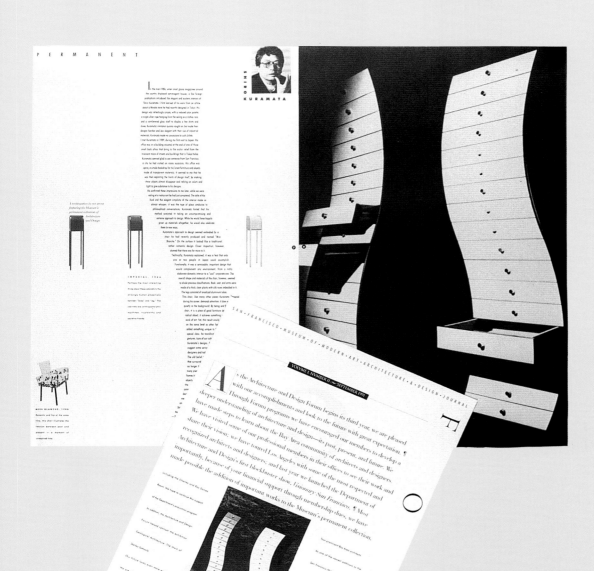

With its use of photos and color screens, and its variety of typefaces, sizes, and column formats, this newsletter's design effectively conveys the nature of the modern art museum for which it is produced.

Utopia
Promotional Packet

DESIGN FIRM
Ideas
(San Francisco, California)

ART DIRECTOR
Robin Brandes

ILLUSTRATOR
John Hersey

CLIENT
Hammersly Technology Partners

Black and yellow inks are given full-bleed coverage with this promotional folder and inserts prepared for a developer of computer software. Only the reversed-out type on the folder's interior reveals the white paper stock that was used.

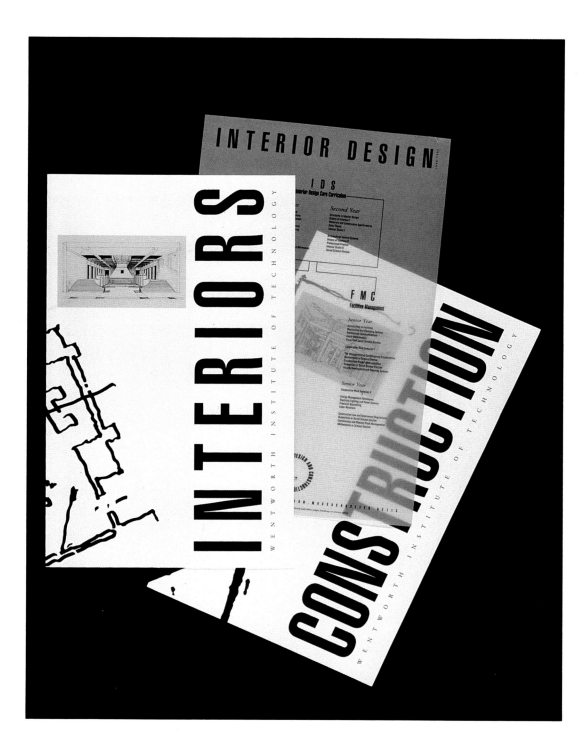

Wentworth Institute of Technology
Brochures

DESIGN FIRM
Clifford Selbert Design
(Cambridge, Massachusetts)

ART DIRECTORS
Clifford Selbert, Robin Perkins

DESIGNER
Robin Perkins

ILLUSTRATOR
Gabriel Yaari

CLIENT
Wentworth Institute of Technology

A tissue-paper insert printed with black ink on full-bleed yellow provides a nice complement to these brochures prepared for Wentworth Institute of Technology. The brochures themselves effectively mix graphics, varied typefaces and sizes, and black and yellow inks. These brochures were prepared to help Wentworth's College of Design and Construction communicate a recent shift of academic emphasis so it could recruit students interested in attending a highly qualified, progressive institution of design.

S. R. Weiner
Event Calendar

DESIGN FIRM
Eymer Design
(Boston, Massachusetts)

ART DIRECTORS
Douglas Eymer, David Ekizian,
Selene Eymer

DESIGNER
Selene Eymer

CLIENT
S. R. Weiner & Associates

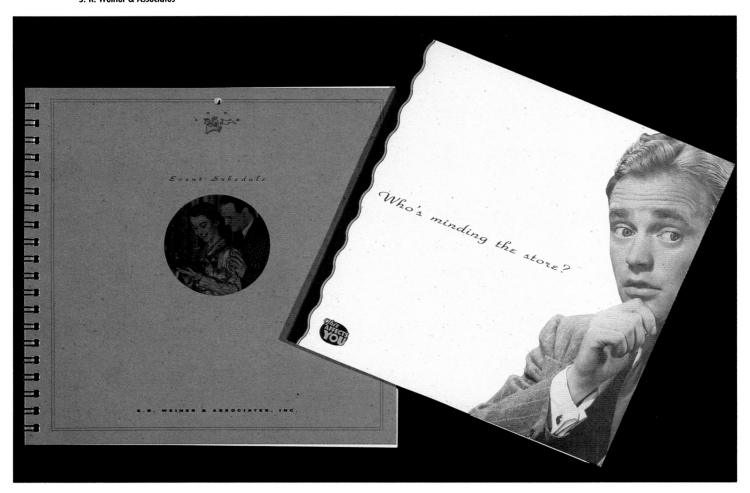

A contemporary format is blended with 1950s-era photos, graphics, and quotations for this calendar commissioned by a shopping mall developer and manager to let retailers know promotional events planned for 1992. By using a different paper for the calendar's covers than for the interior pages, the piece acquires added color.

DESIGN FIRM
JOED Design
(Chicago, Illinois)

ART DIRECTOR
Edward Rebek

DESIGNERS
Joanne Rebek, Andrea Boven,
Edward Rebek

CLIENT
JOED Design

JOED Design used a natural, handmade quality and unusual binding system (a twig, cardboard, and metal wire) to create interest in its promotional brochure. Inside, alternating fake and real duotone images of a hand reaching, stars, a ladder, and finally a hand holding a star suggest the design process and the service the studio provides to its customers.

Greening the Hill:
A Retrospect
Booklet

DESIGN FIRM
Turquoise Design
(Hull, Québec, Canada)

ART DIRECTOR
Mark Timmings

DESIGNER
Mario Godbout

ILLUSTRATOR
Jean Soulard

CLIENT
House of Commons, Canada

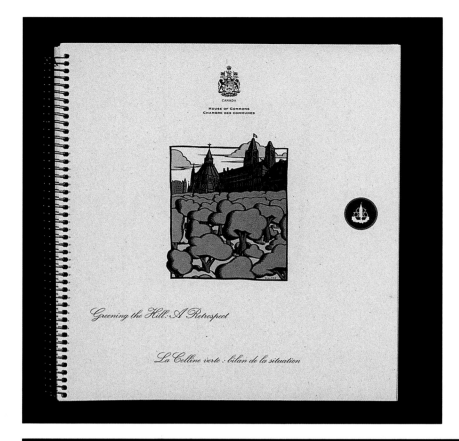

Because this report explores the "greening" of Canada's Parliament Hill, it had to reflect the latest in environmentally friendly production techniques and visual sensitivities. Thus, warm illustrations were used throughout the report, and recycled paper, vegetable-based inks, and metal spiral binding were used in printing.

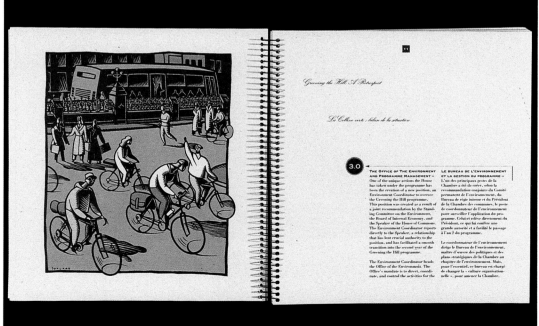

Lux One
Report

DESIGN FIRM
Jerry Takigawa Design
(Pacific Grove, California)

DESIGNERS
Jerry Takigawa, Glenn Johnson

PHOTOGRAPHERS
Paul Caponigro, Huntington Witherill

CLIENT
Center for Photographic Art

The negative
A dreamy progression of opalescent light
Brought to the harsh light of day
In the positive
Soothed by the memory of emotion
Assuming the garb of fluid silver

Negative Print #3, Brewster, New York, 1963

LUX ONE

Lux One was the flagship
publication for the Center
for Photographic Art, a
nonprofit corporation
established to encourage
awareness of photography as
a fine art form. The book
features the work of Paul
Caponigro and Huntington
Witherill. In preparing this
two-color book, Jerry
Takagawa Design selected a
tactile cover stock to help
distinguish the publication.
Special ink draw-downs were
necessary to predict the color
printed on the dark
gray cover.

YMCA of Metropolitan Chicago
Invitation

DESIGN FIRM
Samata Associates
(Dundee, Illinois)

ART DIRECTOR
Pat Samata

DESIGNERS
Pat Samata, Greg Samata

PHOTOGRAPHER
Marc Norberg

CLIENT
YMCA of Metropolitan Chicago

Red and black inks were printed on a yellow cover-weight stock for this invitation to the annual meeting of the YMCA of Metropolitan Chicago. The photo of a child was used as a reference to a speech at the meeting by Chicago Mayor Richard M. Daley entitled "Issues Confronting Chicago's Youth."

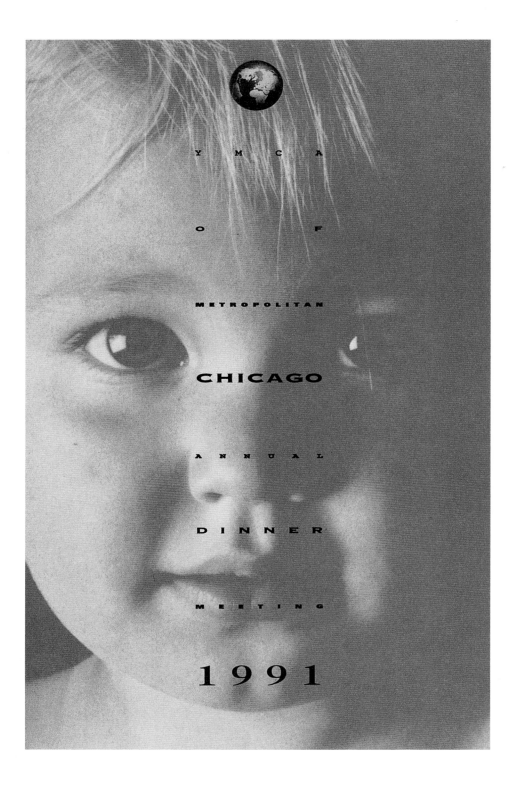

Y M C A

O F

METROPOLITAN

CHICAGO

A N N U A L

D I N N E R

M E E T I N G

1991

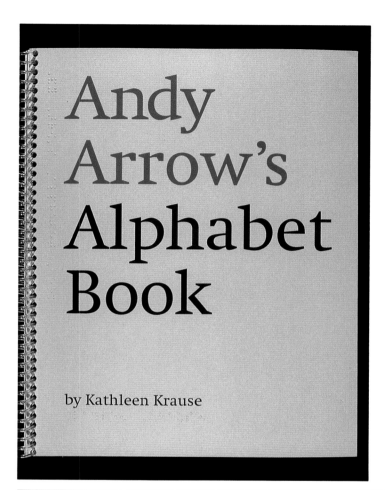

DESIGN FIRM
Thirst
(Chicago, Illinois)

CONCEPT DESIGNER
Kathleen Krause

PROJECT COORDINATORS
Rick Valicenti, Ilse Krause

CLIENT
Kathleen Krause / sponsored by
Gilbert Paper

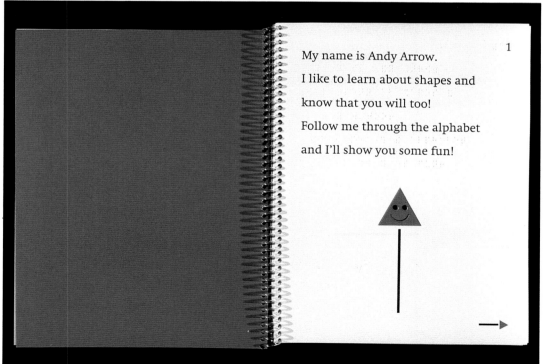

My name is Andy Arrow.
I like to learn about shapes and
know that you will too!
Follow me through the alphabet
and I'll show you some fun!

1

Large type, red and black inks, and illustrations of circles, squares, and triangles help the sighted young reader of this book to understand the geometric shapes that make up the alphabet. What makes this book unique, however, is its use of braille type for all the text, combined with embossing of all the graphics, to help blind readers also understand how the letters of the alphabet look. Creating facsmiles of braille symbols by conventional embossing proved to be a special challenge; previously the only method of braille production had been with a braille machine.

Ontario March of Dimes
Annual Report

DESIGN FIRM
Telmet Design Associates
(Toronto, Ontario, Canada)

ART DIRECTOR
Tiit Telmet

DESIGNERS
Tiit Telmet, Joseph Gault

CLIENT
Ontario March of Dimes

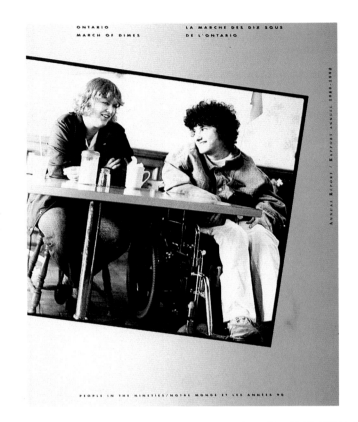

Gradations from light to dark—both with the photographs and the mauve ink—give distinctive beauty to this bilingual annual report for an organization concerned with assisting physically disabled adults. A blend of serif, sans serif, and script types, paired with attractive and easy-to-understand charts, also help make this report successful.

Museum of Science and History
Annual Report

DESIGN FIRM
Robin Shepherd Studios
(Jacksonville, Florida)

ART DIRECTOR
Tom Schifanella

CLIENT
Museum of Science and History

Due to a limited budget, illustrations for this annual report for a Jacksonville museum were generated in-house utilizing steel engravings. The collages were shot as halftones to hold detail. Backgrounds were run separately to control ink gain.

Choosing Design
Report

DESIGN FIRM
Larsen Design Office
(Minneapolis, Minnesota)

ART DIRECTOR
Tim Larsen

DESIGNERS
Mona Marquardt, Marc Kundmann

EDITOR
Charlie Quimby

CLIENT
Core of Understanding Conference
Committee

Choosing Design grew out of the Core of Understanding Conference held in 1989 as a means of bringing the issues discussed at the design-education conference to a wider audience of design educators and students. With a small budget and an enormous amount of material to include, Larsen Design Office prepared this report on its computer, using screen tints, layering, and merging of images to make its pages interesting and readable.

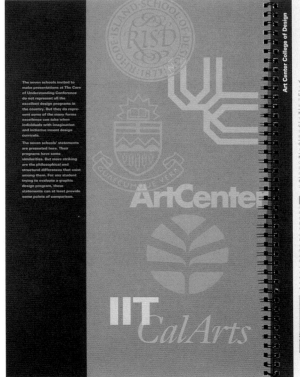

Brainstorm
Report

DESIGN FIRM
Mark Oldach Design
(Chicago, Illinois)

ART DIRECTOR
Mark Oldach

ILLUSTRATOR
David Ciscko

PHOTOGRAPHER
Alan Shortall

CLIENT
USG Interiors

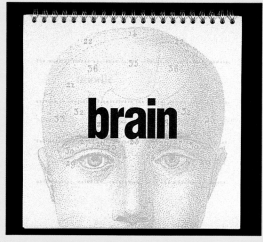

This limited-edition report—
targeted to architects and
interior designers—
promotes a new custom
interiors products service.
The majority of the book
is printed on translucent
paper so that text and image
interact from page to page.
The front cover is printed
with white ink on metal.

IBM Switzerland
Book Jacket

DESIGN FIRM
BBV Baviera
(Zürich, Switzerland)

ART DIRECTOR
Michael Baviera

CLIENT
IBM Switzerland

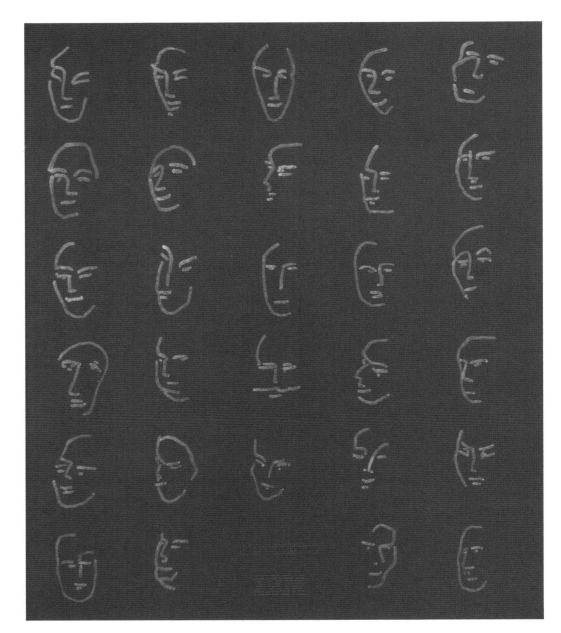

Near solid coverage with blue ink gives force to this jacket for a guidebook by IBM Switzerland. The only other use of color is red ink for the IBM logo and book title at the jacket's base. The various sketches of faces across the cover are produced with reverses to white using fineline offset printing.

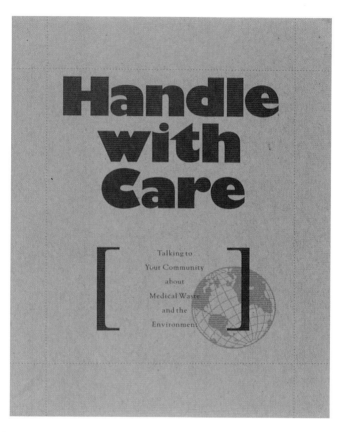

Handle with Care
Report

DESIGN FIRM
Mark Oldach Design
(Chicago, Illinois)

ART DIRECTOR
Mark Oldach

CLIENT
American Hospital Association

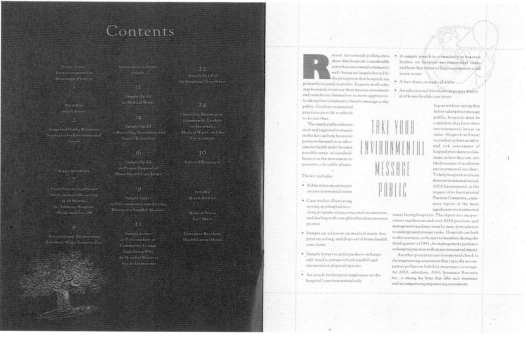

A kraft-colored cover stock, lighter beige interior stock, and brown and purple inks combine to give an attractive, environmental feel to this report on medical waste and the environment. The report is designed to help marketing and public relations professionals understand and communicate local hospitals' environmental concerns to their community.

Massachusetts Horticultural Society
Brochure

DESIGN FIRM
Clifford Selbert Design
(Cambridge, Massachusetts)

ART DIRECTOR
Melanie Lowe, Clifford Selbert

DESIGNER
Melanie Lowe

PHOTOGRAPHER
Harry De Zitter

CLIENT
Massachusetts Horticultural Society

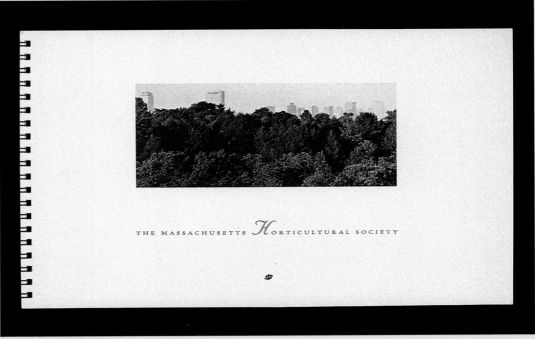

THE MASSACHUSETTS *H*ORTICULTURAL SOCIETY

SUPPORT

This capabilities brochure describes the programs of the Massachusetts Horticultural Society, while also communicating the link between people and nature. It features 300 line-screen duotones, recycled papers, a letterpress cover, and wire-binding for easy updating as programs are added.

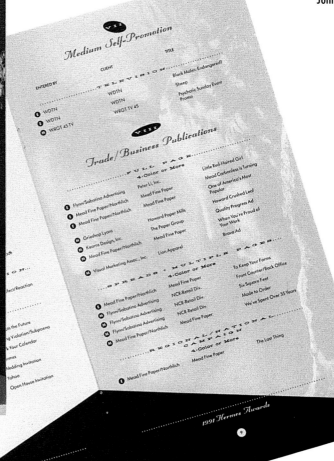

DESIGN FIRM
Visual Marketing Associates
(Dayton, Ohio)

ART DIRECTOR
Kenneth Botts

DESIGNERS
John Walker, Brian Pesti, Kent Miller

PHOTOGRAPHER
Alexander, Glass, Ingersoll

CLIENT
Dayton Advertising Club

The Dayton Advertising Club commissioned Visual Marketing Associates to design and produce a program for its annual Hermes Awards Banquet, recognizing the year's best advertising and design. The booklet lists award winners by category. The graphic form of the front cover is repeated on right-hand pages throughout the program, with the cover photograph ghosted to 10 percent on interior pages.

Mac-D-Caper
Buttons

DESIGN FIRM
Collins & Chu
(Tustin, California)

ART DIRECTORS
Bill Collins, Lorna Moy-Masaki

DESIGNERS
Lorna Moy-Masaki, Johnee Bee

ILLUSTRATOR
Johnee Bee

CLIENT
Ingram Micro

Bright yellow and black colors, and cartoon-style illustrations give personality to the promotional buttons created for a computer software and hardware distributor.

Voters for Choice
Button

DESIGN FIRM
J. Gibson & Company
(Washington, D.C.)

ART DIRECTOR
Gibby Edwards

DESIGNER
Lisa M. Brzezniak

CLIENT
Voters for Choice

This button was a promotional item for a recent concert honoring the anniversary of the *Roe v. Wade* decision of the U.S. Supreme Court. The program featured various performers— political speakers, singers / musicians, and a comedian / political satirist. This button's graphic mark incorporated the three types of performers, with an emphasis on the voices.

Red Tomato
Identity

DESIGN FIRM
JOED Design
(Chicago, Illinois)

ART DIRECTOR
Edward Rebek

DESIGNERS
Joanne Rebek, Ed Rebek

CLIENT
Joe DiVenere / Red Tomato

Bright red and green—the colors of a tomato—are combined with black in this zesty graphic identity for an Italian restaurant and deli. The casual hand script, varying letter scale, vertical "RED," and cartoonesque Italian plum tomato "O" were all developed by JOED Design to help the restaurant convey an image of "food as fun."

THE SOIL WAS WORKED
ITS SEEDLING NURTURED
AND TIME HAS BROUGHT FORTH A

RED TOMATO ™

IT'S FRESH, RIPE
AND READY TO EAT

Guthrie's at the Earth Exchange
Identity

DESIGN FIRM
Annette Harcus Design
(Double Bay, New South Wales, Australia)

ART DIRECTOR
Annette Harcus

DESIGNER
Kristin Thieme

ILLUSTRATORS
Kristin Thieme, Melinda Dudley

CLIENT
Guthrie's at the Earth Exchange

Brown-toned papers, mining-related illustrations, and a dominant use of black ink with touches of blue and rust on some pieces give an appropriately earthy and fun feel to this identity package for a restaurant in a mining museum.

Hogan's Market
Identity

DESIGN FIRM
Hornall Anderson Design Works
(Seattle, Washington)

ART DIRECTORS
Jack Anderson, Julia LaPine

DESIGNERS
Jack Anderson, Julia LaPine,
Denise Weir, Lian Ng

ILLUSTRATOR
Larry Jost

CLIENT
Puget Sound Marketing Corporation

The Hogan brothers were committed to creating a store image that they would be proud to put their family name on. Hornall Anderson Design Works developed this graphic identity to project what the Hogans saw as their business's chief attributes: a market for the quick and specialty foods desired for today's lifestyles, and a place where quality foods are found at a value that appeals to all customers.

McDill Design
Stationery

DESIGN FIRM
McDill Design
(Milwaukee, Wisconsin)

ART DIRECTORS
Clayton Feller, Michael Dillon,
LuAnn Haas-Williams

DESIGNER
Clayton Feller

PRODUCERS
Jeff Neal, Becky Haas

CLIENT
McDill Design

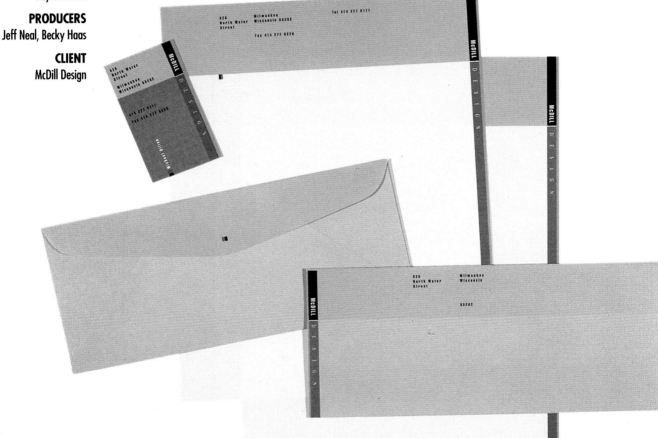

Using the paper's tint as a fourth color, designer Michael Dillon used close registration and strong rectangular blocks to create this stationery system for his design studio. Because its clientele is diverse, the studio wanted an identity with a "reserved dynamism."

DESIGN FIRM
Sonsoles Llorens
(Barcelona, Spain)

ART DIRECTOR
Sonsoles Llorens

CLIENT
J. M. Cuevas & M. L. Alcón /
Arropa Clothes Store

Blue and brown inks and gold stamping are printed on an industrial paper to give a contemporary, eclectic personality to this stationery and shopping bag for a fashionable clothing store.

Streamline Graphics
Stationery

DESIGN FIRM
Evenson Design Group
(Culver City, California)

ART DIRECTOR
Stan Evenson

DESIGNERS
Stan Evenson, Glenn Sakamoto

CLIENT
Streamline Graphics

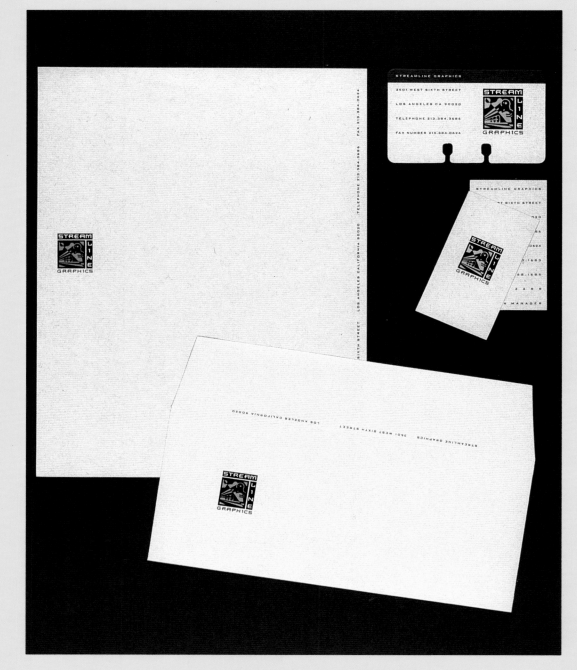

Streamline Graphics was formerly Express Stats. Evenson Design Group renamed the company, then created an image for it that reflected a high-end press plus special-effects vendor. Because the stationery is printed on an earth-toned paper, the white lettering in the company name is created by using a third ink color.

Gotham City Graphics
Stationery

DESIGN FIRM
Gotham City Graphics
(Burlington, Vermont)

ART DIRECTORS
Amey Radcliffe, Stephanie Salmon,
Kathy Yanulavich

CLIENT
Gotham City Graphics

Gotham City Graphics
wanted a look for its
stationery system that would
be "retro" without suggesting
that the studio could only
do that one graphic style.
Linen paper was used to
help bring out the metallic
copper screen used as one
of the three colors.

Colin Edwards Designs
Stationery

DESIGN FIRM
Graphic Ideation Pty
(West Brunswick, Victoria, Australia)

ART DIRECTOR
Tony Mammoliti

ILLUSTRATOR
Chwee Kuan Chan

CLIENT
Colin Edwards Designs

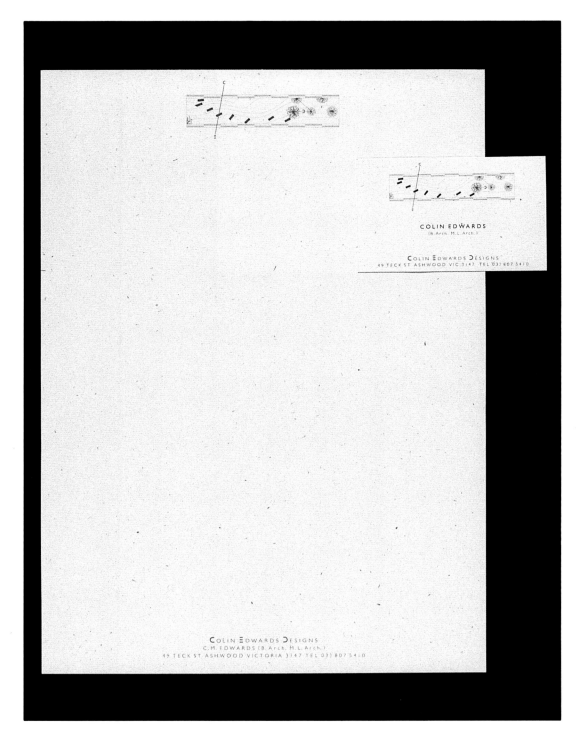

Colin Edwards wanted a graphic symbol for his stationery that would depict landscaping and architecture. Graphic Ideation accomplished this by using a variety of symbols such as scale bars, contours, and natural features. To emphasize respect for the environment, warm gray inks were paired with green on a flecked paper.

Jean Poiré
Stationery

DESIGN FIRM
/erge, LeBel Communication
(Québec, Québec, Canada)

ART DIRECTOR
Marie Rodrigue

DESIGNER
Chantale Audet

CLIENT
Les Agences Jean Poiré Sport

Green and purple serve as standard colors for all elements in this stationery system for a company producing different lines of sportswear. The use of a different third color for the square block on each element lends more colorful variety to the system. The pear (or *poire*, in French) image serves as a graphic reminder of the company name.

Ultra Lucca
Stationery

DESIGN FIRM
Primo Angeli
(San Francisco, California)

ART DIRECTOR
Primo Angeli

DESIGNER
Mark Jones

CLIENT
Lucca Delicatessens

Primo Angeli used the bright, fresh colors of yellow, red, and green (rather than the typical Italian colors of white, red, and green) to develop a graphic look suggesting Ultra Lucca Delicatessens' upbeat atmosphere and fresh food. The embossing added the element of texture, and thus richness, to the stationery.

DESIGN FIRM
Clifford Selbert Design
(Cambridge, Massachusetts)

ART DIRECTOR
Clifford Selbert

DESIGNERS
Clifford Selbert, Liz Rotter

CLIENT
Aolia A. Conrad

This stationery is designed to be expressive of the client's profession, writing. It features her initials in a colorful, whimsical way that alludes to the alphabet. The "A," "d," and "c" were drawn freehand.

Rhonda Francis
Communications
Stationery

DESIGN FIRM
246 Fifth Design Associates
(Ottawa, Ontario, Canada)

ART DIRECTOR
Terry Laurenzio

DESIGNERS
Lisa Lacond, Terry Laurenzio

CLIENT
Rhonda Francis Communications

The design for this stationery
needed to be conservative
while reflecting the client's
personality. In order to keep
the stationery's look simple,
246 Fifth Design Associates
focused on creative use of
typography and bright colors
to get the appropriate
message across.

Todd Ware Massage
Business Card

DESIGN FIRM
The Weller Institute for the Cure of Design
(Park City, Utah)

ART DIRECTOR
Don Weller

CLIENT
Todd Ware Massage

By printing red and yellow atop each other to produce orange, this business card achieves a four-color look despite its use of only three inks (including minimally used black). The idea for the image came from one of Todd Ware's clients, complimenting his "Magic Hands."

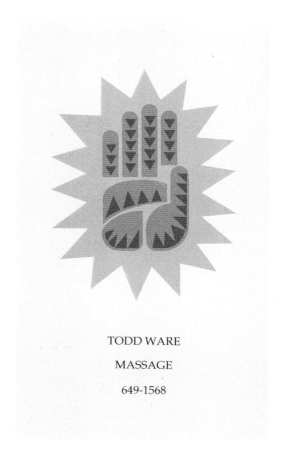

TODD WARE

MASSAGE

649-1568

Iron John Management
Business Card

DESIGN FIRM
Studio without Walls
(North Hollywood, California)

ART DIRECTOR
R&R / Studio without Walls

DESIGNER
Fly

CLIENT
John Axelrod

Iron John Management, an entertainment management firm, wanted a corporate identity suggesting strength, the common man, the digital future, and an industrial feeling. The client particularly liked the way this new logo integrated the firm's initials to form the eye ("I"), jaw ("J"), and man ("M").

Popcorn Book
Self-Promotion

DESIGN FIRM
Evenson Design Group
(Culver City, California)

ART DIRECTOR
Stan Evenson

CLIENT
Evenson Design Group

The Popcorn Report is a book written by Faith Popcorn concerning the future of business in the next 10 to 20 years. Evenson Design Group repackaged the existing book for a holiday promotion. The delicate use of burgundy ink illustrates how minimal usage of a third color can add a subtle but important touch.

HOM Fashion Show
Brochure

DESIGN FIRM
Triumph International
(Hong Kong)

ART DIRECTOR
Catherine Lam Siu Hung

CLIENT
Triumph International (HK) — HOM

Created for a fashion show, this invitation is meant to make one feel how joyful it is to be dressed in the client's clothing. The blue and red figures look like silhouettes below the dark figures when the invitation is closed, then can be seen very clearly once the card is opened—symbolizing a journey from the dull and boring side of life to the world of gaiety and joyfulness made possible by HOM fashions.

Zapata
Catalog

DESIGN FIRM
Concrete Design Communications
(Toronto, Ontario, Canada)

ART DIRECTORS
Diti Katona, John Pylypczak

DESIGNER
Diti Katona

PHOTOGRAPHER
Deborah Samual

CLIENT
Zapata

This promotional catalogue for a clothing designer features a warm-gray graphic print for its cover, with tritone photographs (two shades of black ink, plus gray) on its interior spreads. The catalog was printed on one side only, on one long sheet of paper. This sheet was then accordion-folded and cloth-stitched on the left to create a distinctive booklet.

Kentucky Center
Presents
1990–91 Season
Brochure / Calendar

DESIGN FIRM
Good Design
(Louisville, Kentucky)

DESIGNER
Ruth Wyatt

PHOTOGRAPHER
Richard Bram

CLIENT
Kentucky Center for the Arts

Kentucky Center for the Arts brings performers from around the world for the Kentucky Center Presents series. Good Design's challenges on this project were to combine a brochure and calendar into one piece and to give as much variety and activity as possible to three ink colors. This was done through complex layering of screens and crossing rays of light in the graphic illustrations.

Right at Home
Brochure

DESIGN FIRM
Mark Oldach Design
(Chicago, Illinois)

ART DIRECTOR
Mark Oldach

DESIGNER
Don Emergy

CLIENT
American Hospital Association

Interspersed vertical and horizontal type of varying sizes was blended with red, blue, and green inks to produce this booklet aimed at helping marketing personnel communicate their hospital's role as a community resource for the public. Most of the type throughout the report is sans-serif, with a serif face used for some of the headline type.

Mayer, Brown & Platt
Brochure

DESIGN FIRM
Osborn & DeLong
(Bloomington, Illinois)

CREATIVE DIRECTOR
Doug DeLong

DESIGNER
Victoria Szymcek

ILLUSTRATOR
Toni Hanzon-Kurrasch

CLIENT
Mayer, Brown & Platt

This recruitment brochure was intended to reflect the very traditional values of the Mayer, Brown & Platt law firm. Osborn & DeLong accomplished this look using elements from the classical revival architecture of the firm's headquarters building and a classical page layout as a foundation for text and engraved illustrations.

Community Chest of Hong Kong
Annual Report

DESIGN FIRM
Kan Tai-keung Design & Associates
(Hong Kong)

ART DIRECTOR
Kan Tai-keung

CLIENT
The Community Chest of Hong Kong

The center image on the cover of this annual report is a Chinese New Year's motif meaning "happiness." The corresponding verse further suggests that "It brings happiness when you participate in charity." Throughout the report, halftones printed with black and purple inks are intermixed, as is textual copy in both English and Chinese characters.

GETTING
DOWN TO
BUSINESS

E

ach of our Puget Sound locations
was chosen with a keen eye toward
practicality and convenience.
Wherever you need to be — in the
heart of the city, close to technology
corridors and corporate campuses,
or poised near major residential
areas — we have a locale to save you
time and trouble. ¶ The generous
size of our suites offers other prac-
tical advantages. Two to three times
larger than a hotel room, our residential suites are roomy and private enough to let you conduct in-
terviews, organize meetings, make
presentations and entertain in style.
¶ And our special features, from
spas and exercise rooms to tennis
courts and clubhouses, make it easy
to relax and make yourself at home.

PRACTICALITY

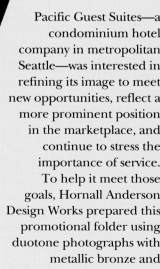

Pacific Guest Suites
Promotional Folder

DESIGN FIRM
Hornall Anderson Design Works
(Seattle, Washington)

ART DIRECTOR
Julia LaPine

PHOTOGRAPHER
Raymond Gendreau

CLIENT
Pacific Guest Suites

Pacific Guest Suites—a
condominium hotel
company in metropolitan
Seattle—was interested in
refining its image to meet
new opportunities, reflect a
more prominent position
in the marketplace, and
continue to stress the
importance of service.
To help it meet those
goals, Hornall Anderson
Design Works prepared this
promotional folder using
duotone photographs with
metallic bronze and
two black inks.

Stella
Poster and Program Booklet

DESIGN FIRM
KROG
(Ljubljana, Slovenia)

ART DIRECTOR
Edi Berk

PHOTOGRAPHER
Tone Stojko

CLIENT
MGL Ljubljana
(Town Theater of Ljubljana)

Written by the German classical playwright Johann Wolfgang Goethe when he was still a student, the tragic love story "Stella" is a typical example of 18th-century middle-class drama. A gold base with red touches adds drama to the poster and the cover of the program booklet. The text pages use black ink only. But distinctive graphics and type, paired with heavy ink coverage and reverses on some spreads, add excitement to the interior design as well.

JOHANN WOLFGANG GOETHE

Prevajalec **Lado Kralj,** Režiser in dramaturg **Janez Pipan,** Lektorica **Majda Križaj,** Scenografa **Dušan Milavec, Boris Benčič,** Kostumografka **Doris Kristić,** Avtor glasbe **Zoran Predin,** Korepetitor **Borut Lesjak,** Asistentka kostumografije **Đurđa Janeš,** Stella **Mirjam Korbar,** Cecilija, spočetka imenovana Madame Sommer **Jožica Avbelj,** Fernando **Slavko Cerjak,** Lucija **Tanja Ribič, k. g.,** Karel **Milan Štefe,** Poštarica **Maja Šugman,** Anica **Barbara Babič, štud. AGRFT,** Kočijaž **Borut Veselko,** Vodja predstave **Marjan Presetnik,** Šepetalka **Cvetka Kernel Račečič,** Tonski tehnik **Stane Bartol,** Lasuljarka **Hermina Pavšin,** Frizerki **Jana Recek, Jelka Leben,** Rekviziterka **Katja Planinc,** Luč **Jože Merhar, Drago Trotošek,** Vodja odrskih del **Nedeljko Ajder,** Tehnični vodja MGL **Janez Lenarčič**

Stella

The Bang Magazine
Promotion

DESIGN FIRM
The Bang Design
(Toronto, Ontario, Canada)

ART DIRECTOR
Bill Douglas

PHOTOGRAPHERS
Anton Corbijn, Richard Moran,
M. K. Studios

CLIENT
The Bang Design Group

Each issue of this new magazine is a separate study in design experimentation. The logo remains constant, as does the overall textured, rich, and very graphic look. But all other elements— color, size, binding, paper stock, etc.—change with each issue. In fact, with issue no. 2, each individual copy was unique, because of varied paper-stock usage. Within each issue, rigid grids are not used. Instead, the look can vary from article to article and page to page.

Compu-Val
Brochure

DESIGN FIRM
Ross Design
(Wilmington, Delaware)

ART DIRECTOR
Tony Ross

DESIGNERS
Tony Ross, Debbie Heaton

CLIENT
Donald Kalil / Compu-Val Investments

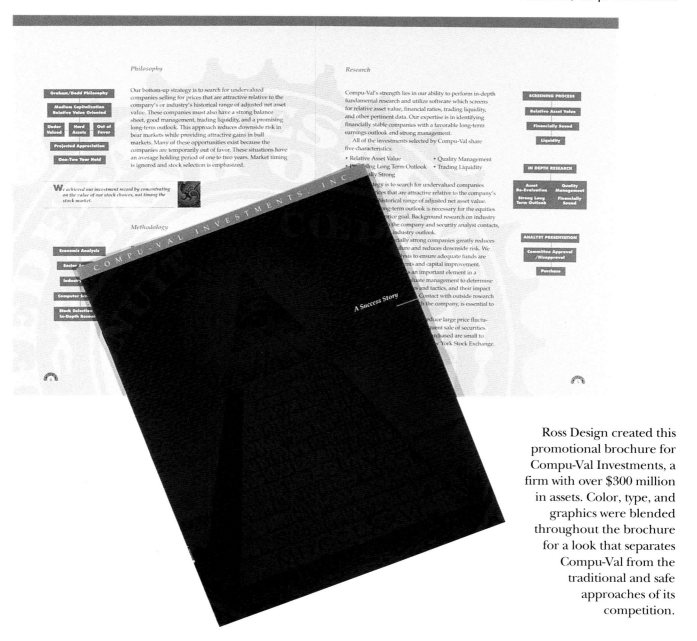

Ross Design created this promotional brochure for Compu-Val Investments, a firm with over $300 million in assets. Color, type, and graphics were blended throughout the brochure for a look that separates Compu-Val from the traditional and safe approaches of its competition.

M. Butterfly
Poster

DESIGN FIRM
Modern Dog
(Seattle, Washington)

ART DIRECTOR
Rich Gerdes / Seattle Repertory
Theatre

DESIGNERS
Michael Strassburger, Robynne Raye

ILLUSTRATOR
Michael Strassburger

CLIENT
Seattle Repertory Theatre

The image for this poster, which advertises a play being staged by a Seattle repertory theater company, was first illustrated with black watercolor. It was then manipulated on a computer to create the split-fountain effect with blue and red inks.

M. BUTTERFLY
by David Henry Hwang

November 27th through December 28th at The Seattle Repertory Theatre.
Tickets 443-2222. Ticketmaster 628-0888.

BLACK POETRY DAY

tumbling blue and brown
tulips that leap
into frogs
women dancing in metal
blue raindrops sliding
into green diamonds
turtles crawling outward
into stars
electric w's
spreading beyond words
papooses turning
into hearts
and butterflies stretching
into court jesters
who jump
amid red splinters
just like you.

- sonia sanchez

OCTOBER 17, 1989

Sponsored by the Clinton-Essex-Franklin Library System. Funded by the New York State Council on the Arts.

Black Poetry Day
Poster

DESIGN FIRM
Creative EDGE
(Burlington, Vermont)

ART DIRECTOR
Rick Salzman

DESIGNERS
Rick Salzman, Barbara Pitfido

CLIENT
Clinton-Essex-Franklin Library System

Black Poetry Day is celebrated across the United States to recognize the achievements of African American writers. Creative EDGE has prepared posters commemorating this day for the Clinton-Essex-Franklin Library System each year since 1984. This poster—with graphics bringing life to the movement expressed in the poem—blends multiple screens of brown, orange, and yellow ink.

David Murray /
Kahil el Zabar
Poster

DESIGN FIRM
Niklaus Troxler
(Willisau, Switzerland)

ART DIRECTOR
Niklaus Troxler

CLIENT
Jazz in Willisau

This silkscreened poster's splatterings of blue, red, and yellow ink creatively form text announcing an upcoming jazz concert in Willisau, Switzerland.

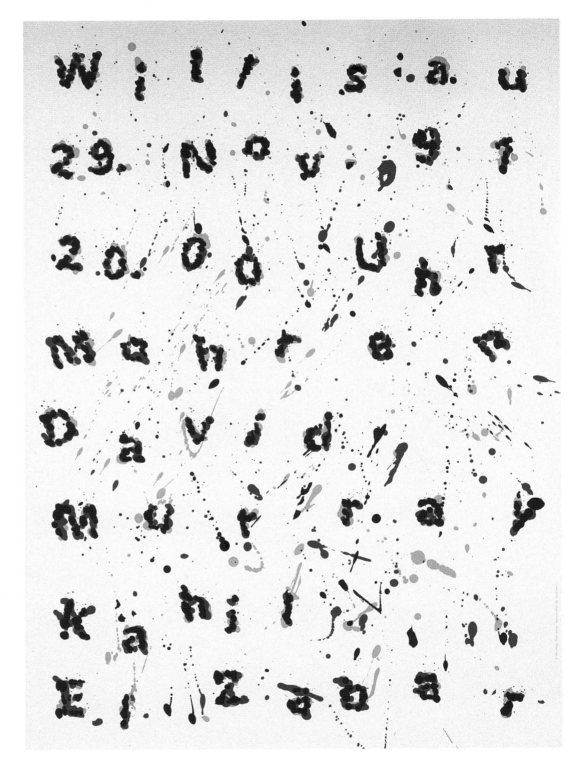

Rynek Sztuki
Poster

DESIGN FIRM
Tadeusz Piechura
(Lódź, Poland)

ART DIRECTOR
Tadeusz Piechura

CLIENT
Rynke Sztuki-Lódź

Small touches of red and blue add delicate color to this poster promoting a "Market of Art." The clients' triangle logo highlights the poster, placed over a halftone of clouds.

South African Jazz Night
Poster

DESIGN FIRM
Niklaus Troxler
(Willisau, Switzerland)

ART DIRECTOR
Niklaus Troxler

CLIENT
Jazz in Willisau

Bold brush-stroke figures of jazz musicians on bright yellow ink strikingly draw attention to this poster promoting a concert in Switzerland of jazz musicians from South Africa. Red ink used for the poster's subtle text adds a delicate third color.

Jazz Meets India
Poster

DESIGN FIRM
Niklaus Troxler
(Willisau, Switzerland)

ART DIRECTOR
Niklaus Troxler

CLIENT
Jazz in Willisau

Free-form strokes of blue
and yellow atop a bright
red base give visual drama to
this poster for a concert
of Indian jazz artists.
By reversing out the textual
type to reveal the white
paper base, the poster
effectually achieves
a fourth color.

Step Reebok IMAGE
Poster

DESIGN FIRM
The Mednick Group
(Culver City, California)

ART DIRECTORS
Scott Mednick, Cheryl Rudich

DESIGNER
Karen Chase

PHOTOGRAPHER
William Hawkes

CLIENT
Reebok International

Reebok International commissioned the Mednick Group design studio to develop this poster as part of an image campaign for the introduction of Step Reebok in the health-club market. A particular challenge in printing this poster was maintaining the density of the copper and black inks across the poster, while also preventing both colors from ghosting and the metallic from printing too light.

Mozart and Salieri
Poster

DESIGN FIRM
KROG
(Ljubljana, Slovenia)

ART DIRECTOR
Edi Berk

CLIENT
MGL Ljubljana
(Town Theater of Ljubljana)

Gold, blue, and black inks
combine to give a celestial
air to this poster advertising
the first production in
Slovenia of one of Alexander
Pushkin's lesser-known plays.
The play analyzes the very
essence of antagonism
between art and craft,
genius and mediocrity,
idea and reality.

Nashville Advertising Federation: Seminar on Advertising Contests
Poster

DESIGN FIRM
Image Design
(Nashville, Tennessee)

DESIGNER
Robert Froedge

CLIENT
Nashville Advertising Federation

This poster was created to generate interest in a lecture about the controversial subject of trade awards. The meeting was held in conjunction with a World War II exhibit, making a war theme appropriate. The earth-toned flecked paper worked with the three inks to serve as a fourth color.

Rush Regatta
Poster

DESIGN FIRM
Sayles Graphic Design
(Des Moines, Iowa)

ART DIRECTOR
John Sayles

CLIENT
University of California,
Santa Barbara

Golden orange, teal blue, and black are the only inks used for this poster/mailer. Creative use of screens, however, produces a multicolored illusion.

USA / USSR
Poster

DESIGN FIRM
Douglas Design
(Tokyo, Japan)

ART DIRECTOR
Douglas Doolittle

CLIENT
Douglas Design

Designer Douglas Doolittle developed this silkscreened poster promoting bilateral disarmament by the United States and the Soviet Union as a promotional piece for his Tokyo studio. The "U" of USA and "S" of USSR are symbolically linked together like a chain.

Equality
Poster

DESIGN FIRM
Douglas Design
(Tokyo, Japan)

ART DIRECTOR
Douglas Doolittle

CLIENT
Douglas Design

This silkscreened promotional poster was intended to focus people's awareness on the imbalance that still exists between men and women. It uses full-bleed coverage of black ink, with reverses for the poster's type.

Hardhat Magazine
Magazine

DESIGN FIRM
Jann Church Partners Advertising
& Graphic Design
(Newport Beach, California)

ART DIRECTORS
Shelly Beck, Jann Church

CLIENT
Fluor Constructors International

Only three colors are used for each issue of the international communications organ for an international industrial construction company. Nevertheless, Jann Church Partners achieves great variety, as well as a consistent identity, both within and among issues by changing the paper stocks and nonblack inks with each issue. Further enhancing the variety are the use of multiple typefaces, diverse grids, and different stocks for the cover and interior pages.

Trends
Promotional Newsletter

DESIGN FIRM
Greer Design Group
(Marietta, Georgia)

ART DIRECTORS
Terry C. Greer, Susan O. Greer

DESIGNERS
John Sillesky

CLIENT
Hopper Paper Company / Georgia Pacific

Because this newsletter serves as a marketing tool for the particular stocks on which it is printed, each issue must illustrate the paper's qualities. One way that Greer Design meets this challenge is stretching to surprising limits the number of apparent colors that can be produced by using screens. Initial issues were printed using only two ink colors. The Winter 1992 issue—illustrated here with an interior spread—was the first with three inks.

Nonni's Biscotti
Packaging

DESIGN FIRM
Bruce Yelaska Design
(San Francisco, California)

ART DIRECTOR
Bruce Yelaska

CLIENT
Nonni's Biscotti

Nonni's Biscotti is a quality
item being sold in a very
competitive market.
Designer Bruce Yelaska used
bright colors and simple
shapes on a bright white bag
to give the package
high visibility and thereby
attract shoppers to it.

DESIGN FIRM
Sayles Graphic Design
(Des Moines, Iowa)

ART DIRECTOR
John Sayles

CLIENT
Central Life Assurance

For an insurance company's trip promotion to Australia, designer John Sayles created a kit with aboriginal-inspired icons, using black, cream, and khaki green inks. Symbols culled from the Australian logo compose a pattern, which is overlaid with hand-lettered copy.

Objectstore
Packaging

DESIGN FIRM
Barrett Design
(Cambridge, Massachusetts)

ART DIRECTOR
Anne Callahan

LOGO DESIGNER
Karen Dendy / ObjectStore

CLIENT
Object Design

ObjectStore is an object-oriented database software package for users in Windows, UNIX, and testing environments. The design was intended to graphically translate the concept of the software. Barrett Design's simple, clean, graphic approach combined bright colors with triangles and circles to emphasize the concept of stored information and distributed objects within a network.

Building Blocks
for Success
Brochure

DESIGN FIRM
Sayles Graphic Design
(Des Moines, Iowa)

ART DIRECTOR
John Sayles

CLIENT
Northwestern University

Sayles Graphic Design created the box for this promotional piece printing purple, rust, and off-white inks on a text-weight gray paper. The printed paper was then laminated (or adhered) to corrugated cardboard and diecut. The accompanying brochure was given a parallel graphic design but printed on a cream-colored 110-lb. cover stock with purple, rust , and gray inks, then diecut and hand-folded to achieve the desired effect.

Student Assistance Scheme Kit
Brochures

DESIGN FIRM
Pierce McDowell Design Management
(Neutral Bay, New South Wales, Australia)

CREATIVE DIRECTOR
Toni McDowell

DESIGNER
Lucy Walker

FINISHING ARTIST
John Bleaney

ILLUSTRATOR
Lucy Walker

CLIENT
Department of Education, Employment,
and Training; Government of Australia

Material in this kit is aimed at youth workers, helping students to apply for financial assistance for continuing studies. Graphics for the kit needed to appeal to both the workers and the students. The theme illustration artwork can be adapted for either full panel or strip usage only—the strip being a diagonal slice through the illustration. The three-color separations for the illustration can also be combined to produce a two-color version when necessary.

Fleet Aerospace
Annual Report

DESIGN FIRM
Concrete Design Communications
(Toronto, Ontario, Canada)

ART DIRECTORS
Diti Katona, John Pylypczak

DESIGNER
Scott A. Christie

CLIENT
Fleet Aerospace Corporation

Metallic and nonmetallic green inks and a tint varnish are merged with subtle screens and, for the text, reverses to white to produce the cover for this annual report for Fleet Aerospace Corporation. The images on the cover are a collage of Fleet's manufacturing operations, including quality approval stamps and an assembled component.

INSURANCE AND THE SEX DISCRIMINATION ACT 1984

$$$

INSURANCE

HUMAN RIGHTS AND EQUAL OPPORTUNITY COMMISSION

1990

DESIGN FIRM
Eymont Kin-Yee Design Pty
(Paddington, New South Wales,
Australia)

ART DIRECTOR
Myriam Kin-Yee

DESIGNER
Sharon Pearson

CLIENT
Human Rights of Australia

Human Rights of Australia
is a federal body involved in
many facets of human rights,
equality, and discrimination
issues. All of these issues
being of a very sensitive
nature, Eymont Kin-Yee's
challenge was to design a
cover that would convey a
message without causing
offense. The studio used a
combination of screens and
illustrations to maximize the
effect of the three colors
of ink used.

Sirius Software
Promotional Folder

DESIGN FIRM
Barrett Design
(Cambridge, Massachusetts)

ART DIRECTOR
Karen Dendy

ASSISTANT DESIGNER
Rob Keohane

CLIENT
Sirius Software

Sirius Software, a start-up software company, was seeking a system of data sheets and a folder to distribute to prospective clients. Graphic textures and features for the folder and sheets were created using drawing software with pattern fills. Because Sirius offers different services and its software has many functions, Barrett Design built upon the folder's basic pattern to develop a system of colors and patterns that differentiate the individual sheets.

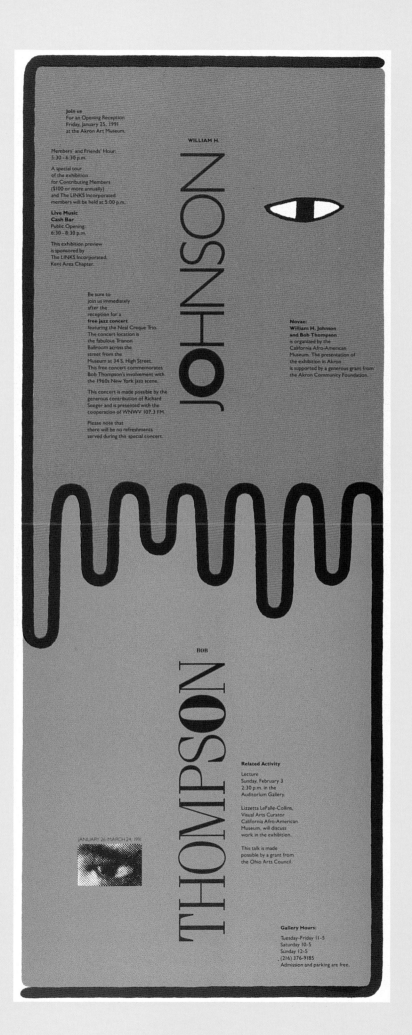

Novae
Invitation

DESIGN FIRM
Epstein, Gutzwiller & Partners
(Cleveland, Ohio)

ART DIRECTOR
Sylvie Allaire

CLIENT
Akron Art Museum

This bright orange, green, and blue announcement invitation had to equally display the stylistic similarities and differences of William H. Johnson and Bob Thompson, two African American artists whose works were being exhibited at the Akron Art Museum. It was printed with matte inks on matte paper.

Savala / Lalicker
Wedding Invitation

DESIGN FIRM
Savala Design
(Anaheim, California)

ART DIRECTOR
Cheryl Savala

CLIENT
Cheryl Savala

Designer Cheryl Savala's challenge was to prepare a cost-effective invitation to her wedding. Her solution was a double-flap folding invitation that would hold the reply card inside. The typography guided the reader on a journey of exciting graphics that created a fun, party-like mood.

A Tasty Affair
Invitation

DESIGN FIRM
Jerry Takigawa Design
(Pacific Grove, California)

ART DIRECTOR
Jerry Takigawa

DESIGNERS
Jerry Takigawa, LeAnn Hansen

PHOTOGRAPHER
Martin Takigawa

CLIENT
KAZU-FM, Monterey Bay Public Radio

From Kazu FM

A Special Invitation

A Celebration

A Night To Remember

A Tasty Affair

Sunday, November 4, 1990

At The Monterey Plaza Hotel

Tasting From 5.00 To 8.00 PM

Followed By Terry Hanck

And The Soul Rockers

"A Tasty Affair" is a fundraising wine and food event for listener-supported radio station KAZU. The photographic approach was created while viewing 35mm contact sheets, which had been photocopied, under an 8X loupe. Under the loupe, the images appeared like charcoal drawings. Jerry Takigawa Design rephotographed the photocopied contact sheet and enlarged the results. Gold ink was substituted for the highlighted areas.

The Wright Night
Invitation

DESIGN FIRM
Platinum Design
(New York, New York)

ART DIRECTOR
Victoria Peslak Hyman

DESIGNER
Kirsten Schumacher

CLIENT
American Craft Museum

This invitation was designed for a retrospective exhibition on Frank Lloyd Wright for the American Craft Museum. It was produced in Wright's favorite colors and used as its central element a photograph of a chair he designed. Printing the invitation on a translucent vellum stock proved challenging.

FSA "Boldly into Tomorrow"
Invitation

DESIGN FIRM
Hornall Anderson Design Works
(Seattle, Washington)

ART DIRECTOR
Jack Anderson

DESIGNERS
Jack Anderson, Jani Drewfs,
David Bates

CLIENT
Food Services of America

Hornall Anderson Design Works created these materials to produce interest in a conference for food service vendors/customers. The conference was sponsored by Food Services of America, an institutional food distributor, and was focused on exploring a breakthrough concept in partnership through which FSA and the buyers could work in the future.

Doesn't that Just Stink?
Christmas Promotion

DESIGN FIRM
Parham-Santana
(New York, New York)

ART DIRECTORS
John Parham, Maruchi Santana

CLIENT
Parham-Santana

This 1990 Christmas promotion was Parham-Santans's corporate gift for that year. The studio decided that, instead of giving fancy gifts to its clients, it would give donations to an organization involved with rainforest conservation. The promotion was silkscreened on recycled chipboard, with a pine-scented and -shaped air freshener attached. The air freshener was purchased at an auto supply store and hung from a metal grommet punched into the chipboard.

Ciudad de los Niños
Invitation

DESIGN FIRM
Rossana Hodoyan
(Tijuana, Baja California, México)

ART DIRECTOR
Rossana Hodeyan

CLIENT
Asociación para los Niños de Tijuana, A.C.

Designer Rossana Hodoyan prepared this attractive invitation for the inauguration of "Ciudad de los Niños" (City of Children)—a private association that works to give street children housing, families, and education.

Hotel Crescent Court
Press Kit Labels

DESIGN FIRM
Hilary Hudgens Design
(Dallas, Texas)

ART DIRECTOR
Hilary Hudgens

DESIGNER
Greg Morgan

CLIENT
Hotel Crescent Court

These labels using metallic copper and burgundy and nonmetallic black inks were used to seal a press kit box containing hotel literature and brochures. The labels reveal awards won by the hotel while capturing an empirical and international feel. All line work and typography were produced on a computer, with color separations done by hand.

Horoscope
Postcards

DESIGN FIRM
Cat Lam
(Hong Kong)

ART DIRECTOR
Catherine Lam Siu Hung

CLIENT
Card Gallery

These art-gallery postcards dramatically depict the various signs of the Zodiac. The basic design is simple but strongly reflects the style and taste of the designer. The red cards are printed with only red inks, with screens used to create the pink figures. The yellow cards are printed with three ink colors and also utilize screens for some of the background figures.

Green
346

Yellow
105

INDEX BY ART DIRECTOR & DESIGNER

Count Your Life
With Smiles

"Count Your Garden by the Flowers
Never by the leaves that fall
Count Your Days by Golden Hours
Don't remember the clouds at all.

Count Your Nights by Stars, not shadows
Count Your Life with Smiles, not tears
And with Joy through all Your Lifetime
Count Your Age by Friends, not years."

Inscribed

_____

BW